ישיבה תורת חיים

Yeshiva Toras Chaim
Talmudical Seminary/Denver

1400 Quitman Street • P.O. Box 4067
Denver, Colorado 80204
(303) 629-8200

Toras Chaim: Perpetuating our Heritage

The heritage and strength of the Jewish people has always been the precious Torah, which forms the foundation of Jewish life and spirit. The concept of Torah study is not an endeavor limited to any specific moment or location, but rather a primary objective in Jewish living at any time and in any place.

"Study is the life-breath of the Jewish people, the goal of Jewish existence—its purpose and destiny," stated the sainted Rabbi Aaron Kotler, teacher and mentor of the men who head Yeshiva Toras Chaim Talmudical Seminary/Denver. Jewish life stands and falls in the measure of its devotion to study. It is the devotion of scholars which provides the life-blood of Jewish existence even to those limbs which are far removed from the heart. The survival and eternity of Jewish peoplehood depend on the development and growth of scholars. It is they who transmit our spiritual heritage from generation to generation. Without scholars, Jewry lacks the men of wisdom who are the links in the great chain of tradition spanning the ages; and it lacks the educators to instruct the coming generations in the purity and perfection of our eternal tradition.

Yeshiva Toras Chaim Talmudical Seminary/Denver was founded in 1967 on the solid rock of Torah precepts. It was the first Yeshiva high school and college level Hebrew studies program between the Mississippi River and the West Coast. With its foundation firmly entrenched in Torah, Yeshiva Toras Chaim began its upward growth. From that fledgling state, the Yeshiva had grown to a formidable institution.

Over the years, Yeshiva Toras Chaim has demonstrated devotion and commitment—a commitment, not only to the individual development and spiritual growth of each student, but a commitment to transmit our special heritage to Jewish youth, young community leaders, professionals, educators, and businessmen, as well.

Recently, the Yeshiva responded rapidly to an urgent appeal and accepted four young Russian students. The young men came from Moldavia, U.S.S.R. They arrived under a special student exchange program, and the Yeshiva had accepted full educational and financial responsibility for them.

In order to extend its educational horizons, Yeshiva Toras Chaim offers varied Torah learning programs which appeal to many segments of Denver's Jewish community. A wellspring of Torah knowledge is available at the Yeshiva which is unparalleled in Denver. Jewish scholars share their knowledge with those who wish to find their Jewish roots or expand their Jewish intellectual horizons.

Yeshiva Toras Chaim is proud to participate in the publication of this special exclusive edition of Chaim Shlomo Friedman's *Dare to Survive*, a moving autobiographical account of spiritual heroism during the dark days of the Holocaust. We hope this book will help to increase the awareness of the suffering and plight of the Holocaust victims, and serve as a reminder of the struggle of our people for so many generations. We trust you and your family will find this book a source of Torah inspiration and personal edification.

Published and distributed
in the U.S., Canada and overseas by
C.I.S. Publishers and Distributors
180 Park Avenue, Lakewood, New Jersey 08701
(908) 905-3000 Fax: (908) 367-6666

Distributed in Israel by
C.I.S. International (Israel)
Rechov Mishkalov 18
Har Nof, Jerusalem
Tel: 02-538-935

Distributed in the U.K. and Europe by
C.I.S. International (U.K.)
89 Craven Park Road
London N15 6AH, England
Tel: 01-809-3723

Book and cover design: Deenee Cohen
Typography: Nechamie Miller

Cover illustration reproduced
from original painting by Francis McGinley

ISBN 1-56062-135-4

CHAIM SHLOMO FRIEDMAN

DARE
TO
SURVIVE

———————————•———————————

ABRIDGED EDITION

CIS

P·U·B·L·I·S·H·E·R·S

New York · London · Jerusalem

Dedicated in Memory
of
Those Who Paved the Way

◆◆◆◆◆◆◆◆◆◆◆◆◆◆◆◆◆◆◆◆

מוקדש לזכר נשמות

ר' אשר ב"ר אברהם יעקב ז"ל — אדאלף
נפטר י"א ניסן תשל"ו

✦ ✦ ✦ ✦

ר' ניסן ב"ר אברהם מרדכי ז"ל — רינגעל
נפטר כ"ט תשרי תשט"ו

ר' דוד ב"ר משה צבי ז"ל — ווערטענטייל
נפטר כ"ט שבט תשל"ט

מרת העׂנא מרים בת ר' אברהם דוב ע"ה — רינגעל
נפטרה ב' כסלו תשכ"ד

מרת טילא בת ר' חיים יעקב ע"ה — ווערטענטייל
נפטרה כ"ד אב תרצ"ט

מרת רבקה בת ר' אהרן דוד הכהן ע"ה — אדאלף
נפטרה ג' חשון תשל"א

מרת ליבא רבקה בת ר' משה דוד ע"ה — כ"ץ
נפטרה י"ב אב תשי"ג
יהי זכרם ברוך

הנאהבים והנעימים בחייהם, ובמותם לא נפרדו

על ידי
ניסן וליבא רינגעל

Dedicated in Honor
of
Those Who Continue to Pave the Way

❖❖❖❖❖❖❖❖❖❖❖❖❖❖❖❖❖❖❖❖

Our Dear Parents

ר׳ אברהם וחנה רינגעל שליט״א

מרת מרים אדאלף שתח׳

וכל מי שעוסקים בצרכי צבור באמונה,
הקדוש ברוך הוא ישלם שכרם ...
וישלח ברכה והצלחה בכל מעשה ידיהם ...

Nissan and Leba Ringel
Rivki, Usher Dovid,
Moshe Tzvi,
Zecharia Elimelech,
Aron and Shneur Zalman

RABBINAAT

van de

ISRAELITISCHE ORTHODOXE GEMEENTE

"MACHSIKE HADASS"

JACOB JACOBSSTRAAT 22 - 2018 ANTWERPEN

Rabbi Chaim Kreiswirth

Chief Rabbi of Antwerp, Belgium

בס״ד

Antwerp, *Rosh Chodesh Kislev*, 5746/1985

I am delighted that my dear friend Rabbi Chaim Shlomo Friedman is publishing a book recalling the dreadful events of the holocaust. I am convinced that every holocaust survivor, each a "firebrand saved from the flames," will find these memoirs to be a reflection of his own experiences.

I have known the author for many years, and I can attest with full confidence that all his writings are the unadorned truth, without omission or addition.

Chaim Kreiswirth
Chief Rabbi of Antwerp

APPROBATION TO THE YIDDISH-LANGUAGE EDITION
PUBLISHED BY THE AUTHOR HIMSELF DURING HIS LIFETIME

TABLE OF CONTENTS

———————————◼———————————

PUBLISHER'S NOTE

—————————————◼—————————————

T HE QUINTESSENTIAL IMAGE OF THE HOLOCAUST IS A long line of terrified Jewish men, women and children being herded into the gas chambers by sadistic Nazi guards and snarling dogs in the shadow of watchtowers and barbed wire. But this was only the final step in the monstrous German genocidal attack on their innocent Jewish victims. It was preceded by a carefully designed strategy of dispossession, degradation, disorientation, duplicity, treachery, terror, forced labor, mayhem, indiscriminate murder, deportation, ghettos, round-ups and liquidations—all executed with fiendish Germanic efficiency and brutality—so that when the Jews were finally transported to the concentration camps they were already physically and emotionally exhausted, numb with grief, dazed and defeated.

In *Dare to Survive*, the third volume in *The Holocaust Diaries*, Rabbi Chaim Shlomo Friedman relates his own experiences in the ghettos and labor camps in the environs of Cracow in southern Poland, followed by his flight to the illusory safety of Slovakia and Hungary. Although the author himself was never deported to the concentration camps, he experienced every step of the tragedy-filled process that led up to deportation, and only through the most phenomenal tenacity and resourcefulness, as well as numerous miraculous escapes, did he manage to avoid being inextricably trapped in the web of the Nazi spider.

Dare to Survive was originally written in Yiddish and first published in 1985 in a Yiddish-language edition, under the title *Ich Vell Zei Iberleiben*, shortly before the author passed away on 25 *Tishrei* of that year at the age of seventy-two. In 1987, it was translated into Hebrew by Yitzchak Eizik Ovitz, re-edited and published in Eretz Yisrael under the title *Lo Amus Ki Echyeh*. The present English-language edition was translated from the edited Hebrew version by Avraham Yaakov Finkel and subsequently underwent further painstaking editing. However, because this volume is being published posthumously, and because we were very careful not to compromise the extraordinary authenticity of the work by unauthorized additions and embellishments, we were restricted in the kinds of clarifications and adjustments that could be incorporated into the text itself. Moreover, due to his characteristic humility and self-effacement, the author would never have agreed to write about himself some of the things that need to be said. Therefore, the burden of presenting some important clarifications falls to these prefatory publisher's remarks.

As the reader progresses through this amazing memoir,

he will be impressed by the uncanny ring of truth of the author's words. The author has clearly attempted to record the unadorned facts to the best of his recollection, utterly devoid of any heroic posturing or self-aggrandizement. Yet in spite of his efforts, a very sharp characterization of the author emerges from these pages with great force, a portrait of a man with unusual physical, mental, emotional and spiritual qualities, a tenacious fighter with the heart of a lion and the soul of a saint.

At the outbreak of the war, the author seems to have been leading a very idyllic Jewish life. At the time, he was a young, gregarious Belzer *chassid,* with beard and *peyos* and the traditional *chassidic* garb, completely absorbed in the communal Belzer dedication to Torah, *avodah* and *gemillus chassadim.* He had a young wife and an infant daughter, as well as an elderly mother and several brothers. He also seems to have been reasonably well off. As the war began, however, his entire life collapsed; flight and the search for a safe haven became his overriding concern. But the rapid onslaught of the German invasion of Poland sealed his avenues of escape at every turn, and there was no choice left but to dig in and try to survive under the yoke of the Nazi oppressor.

As time went on, the near impossibility of this endeavor became increasingly clear. Virtually every day, there were new oppressive Nazi edicts, full of cunning and deceit, designed to crush the spirit of the trapped Jewish people as the noose was drawn slowly, inexorably and ever more tightly around their necks. In this desperate situation, the author's natural penchant for defiance and independent thinking prevented him from being swept along in the carefully engineered mass attitudes and protected him from the false sense of security and the disorientation that were deliberately planted among the Jews by the Germans in the psychological phase of their attack on the Jewish people. He did not grant the Nazis even the smallest modicum of credibility, refusing to accept anything at face value. If everyone was running to take advantage of a new opportunity that suddenly seemed to present itself, he would hang back in wary distrust, an attitude that saved his life numerous times. He became an insatiable sponge for information, ever alert, ever vigilant, his antennae always attuned to the slightest rumor, constantly evaluating his findings and seeking the tiny grain of truth amidst the overwhelming dross of disinformation and fantasy.

When he did find that tiny opening in the Nazi net, he never vacillated but plunged forward with resolute determination, great personal courage and an utter lack of fear. Extremely resourceful and persuasive, he felt very confident in his ability to wriggle his way out of any tight spot, and this confidence was continually tested.

With frustrating regularity, however, one escape attempt after another ended in failure, but he was not discouraged or disheartened. Buttressed by his stanch faith in Hashem, he would simply accept his temporary defeat with humility and grace as *gam zu letovah* and forge on to the next scheme, hopeful that perhaps in this new attempt Hashem would grant him success. And when, time and time again, he miraculously eluded the hungry hand of death, he never attributed his deliverance to blind happenstance or his own formidable abilities but to divine benevolence, which he acknowledged with humble gratitude. Never did he become an instinctive, cornered animal fighting for survival without heart, without soul.

In one memorable episode, he was standing in a railway station, part of a large crowd of captured Jews heading for an unknown fate, when he saw a man of his acquaintance and felt certain that the man was penniless. In that terrifying predicament, he had the presence of mind and the compassionate impulse to take up a collection among the other captives so that the man would not feel utterly lost. Yet the author's description of this episode is brief and matter-of-fact, as if such a remarkable act of kindness and compassion is nothing more than is to be expected under the circumstances. Clearly, this was a man of rare and outstanding personal qualities, an exemplary *baal madreigah* who refused to posture for the reader. Indeed, quite often throughout the book, the reader may be struck by the author's reticence about his feelings and emotions, but although we have scrupulously avoided inserting such passages into the text, the discerning reader will find the author's innermost feelings occasionally bursting through in a flash of emotion, which is then quickly suppressed.

It is also quite clear that it must have taken tremendous physical strength and stamina for the author to endure all the brutal beatings he suffered at the hands of the Nazis on numerous occasions and to be able to pick himself up and continue undaunted in his desperate struggle for survival. The author also must have had enormous reservoirs of energy and endurance to withstand the constant long marches, privations, hunger and sleeplessness in relatively vigorous good health.

All in all, we are presented with the image of a man of truly heroic proportions in a very Jewish sense, powerful and fearless but non-violent, deeply pious and compassionate, driven by dedication to the highest ideals of the Torah, vastly resourceful but humbly subservient to and accepting of the divine will. And yet, in spite of all his remarkable ability, many

manifestly miraculous incidents played key roles in his ultimate survival.

In this light, we are presented with a very convincing
explanation of one of the more puzzling aspects of the
holocaust. People often ask: Why didn't the Jews resist? Why
did they allow themselves to be led like sheep to the slaughter? The answer is clearly that the Jews were overwhelmed
and crushed by the enormity and scope of the merciless Nazi
assault so graphically depicted in *Dare to Survive*. Only the
strongest and most audacious people could even dream of
evading the Nazis, and often, even those were only able to
survive through manifestly miraculous intervention, as the
author's experience demonstrates. Most ordinary people,
however, were simply incapable of such heroic escapades.
The infernal Nazi trap was cleverly and diabolically sprung,
and there was simply nothing to do, nowhere to turn. But in
their final hours, the Jewish victims—especially those imbued
with Torah values—found within themselves a deeper and
greater heroism. Bowing their heads to the inevitability of
their destiny, they separated themselves from their tormentors by a veil of holiness, and they resolved to give up their
lives *al kiddush Hashem*. In the end, although overcome by an
unspeakably profound grief and dread for themselves and
their loved ones, they still went to their deaths with pride and
dignity, never lowering themselves to the bestial level of their
accursed tormentors.

In one illuminating passage from the book, the author
receives a final message from his mother in which she says,
"I'm well aware of what they are going to do to us. I have only
minutes to live, but I'm not afraid to die. I am going to my
death as if I were going to a wedding. I am happy mainly
because I have been granted the *zchus* of marrying off my

children the way I have always hoped for, to decent, Torah-observant husbands and wives. I am also happy that my son Chaim Shlomo . . . managed to escape from the ghetto . . ." Paradoxically, at the time this gallant woman sent her final message, the children she was so proud of having married off properly had already gone to their final destiny, and yet, she did not feel it had all been for naught. Rather, she felt an abiding sense of accomplishment for having fulfilled her duties as a Jewish mother. Her life had been fully dedicated to the Creator and His Torah, and even the slaughter of her entire family could not take this away from her. This was heroism of a much higher order, and such heroes and heroines were far beyond the reach of the Nazis. The Nazis could kill them, but they could not defeat them.

Unfortunately, not all Jews were cut from this noble cloth. Many Jews of a baser nature, motivated by greed and the spurious assurance of personal safety, became the tools of the Nazis in the perfidious deception, oppression and deportation of the Jewish people through the infamous Judenrats (Nazi-installed Jewish community councils) and the Jewish police. In a very important aspect of his eyewitness testimony, the author angrily accuses these ruthless men, drunk with their Nazi-endowed power, of deliberately misleading, brutalizing, plundering, cheating and betraying their own people. The author points out, however, that none of these men were Torah-observant Jews, although some came from Torah-observant homes, which only underscores that the Torah has a tremendous power to elevate a person and protect him from his darker side, that what ultimately separates the Jew from his barbaric oppressors is the mantle of the holy Torah.

The author received his mantle of the holy Torah in the hallowed environment of Polish *chassidus*. His grandfather

Rabbi Reuven Friedman was an outstanding *talmid chacham* and a *chassid* of the Radomsker Rebbe (author of *Tiferes Shlomo*), and his father Rabbi Elyakim Friedman was a similarly outstanding *talmid chacham* and a *chassid* of the Zhabner Rav (author of *Yad Shalom*). The author himself, who lost his father at a very young age, felt strongly attracted to the rapidly growing and dynamic Belzer *chassidus*, and as a fifteen-year-old boy, he travelled to Belz where he studied diligently for the next five years. Afterwards, he always remained a devoted Belzer *chassid*, and he maintained a close association with Belzer Rebbe for the rest of his life. In *Dare to Survive*, the author describes his role in the Belzer Rebbe's dramatic escape from Poland and their moving reunion in Budapest before the Belzer Rebbe went on to Eretz Yisrael. Indicative of what lay close to his heart, the author closes his narrative with an account of his activities in helping the Belzer Rebbe establish the world-renowned network of Belzer *yeshivos* in the aftermath of the war.

The publication of *Dare to Survive*, closely following the publication of *Late Shadows* by Moshe Holczler and *They Called Me Frau Anna* by Chana Marcus Banet, is a significant milestone for the *Holocaust Diaries* collection. We feel that it is a great *zchus* and honor to have presented volumes of such stature to the public, as each of these works, in its own way, depicts the nobility of spirit and the deeper heroism of the Jewish people in the darkest chapter of their history. A fourth volume is scheduled for release later this winter, two more volumes are in advanced stages of preparation, and several more are in the planning stages.

In closing, I would like to extend a note of acknowledgment to Rabbi Avraham Yaakov Finkel for his highly professional and meticulous efforts in the translation of this work

16

and to Editorial Director Raizy Kaufman for her scrupulous preservation of the integrity and authenticity of the entire book. I would also like to extend a note of gratitude to our entire staff who labored vigorously and devotedly in the production of this distinguished book. We all feel that autobiographical accounts such as these are an inestimable legacy for all future generations, and we are humbly grateful to the *Ribono Shel Olam* for granting us the privilege of participating in this important work.

Y.Y.R.
Lakewood, N.J.
Marcheshvan 5752

DARE
TO
SURVIVE

CHAPTER 1

———————————■———————————

Expulsion from Cracow

WHEN GERMANY INVADED POLAND ON SEPTEMBER 1, 1939, the peaceful existence of the Jewish community of Cracow was forever shatterd. During the first year of the occupation, we suffered through one harsh another, but somehhow, we mangaed to cling to a faint semblance of normalcy in our lives. But then it all changed.

It happened during the summer, about one year after the German invasion. Yellow posters, harbingers of new evil Nazi decrees, appeared all over the city. What would it be this time? Horror-stricken, the Cracow Jews read the ominous lines. Not in their worst nightmares could they have thought of this. The proclamation, signed by Governor General Frank, stated that Cracow was to be rendered *Judenrein*, free of Jews, with the exception of the Padgursz district where a ghetto was to be erected to hold no more than ten thousand Jews. No date was set for the implementation of the directive.

Immediately, overtures were made to have the decree rescinded, but it was to no avail. There were Jews who had influence with the Gestapo, but Governor-General Frank was inaccessible. He despised the Jews and would not allow a Jew to get near him. The Jews of Cracow were despondent; sixty thousand people were to be exiled to an unknown destination, forced to leave behind their homes, their businesses, their possessions.

The summer went by, and the expulsion order was not carried out. However, early in the winter of 1941 the Germans turned to the Judenrat, instructing it to set the operation into motion. The members of the Judenrat diligently set out to do their job. As an initial step they sent notices to all Cracow Jews notifying them that by a certain date they were to leave the city. Any non-compliance would be dealt with severely.

Of course, at the top of the expulsion list were the poor and members of the middle class. Since only ten thousand Jews were permitted to remain in the ghetto, priority went to members of the Judenrat and their families. Next in line were the rich who paid huge sums of money for the "privilege" of remaining in the ghetto. The whole affair turned into an enormous financial windfall for the leaders of the Judenrat, who selfishly considered only the profits that could be realized from this expulsion.

Since the expelled Jews were not overly anxious to comply with the expulsion order, the Judenrat and the Jewish police began to use harsh measures to enforce it, entering homes and carting off the inhabitants by brute force.

Like all Cracow Jews, my mother and my older brother

Pesachyah who lived with her also received eviction notices. Afraid that they might come and drag her out of bed in the middle of the night, she came to sleep in my house. It was just around that time that my wife gave birth to a baby girl. I wrote a letter to the Judenrat, requesting a postponement of my departure date, since it would be impossible to travel with a newborn infant during the cold winter months. Granting my request, they gave me an extension for one month. The days flew by, and fearing that they might evict me by force, I moved into my mother's apartment hoping to be safe there, since her house had not been raided for a long time. I continually stayed on the move, trying to evade them, but I miscalculated badly. The Judenrat had ways of dealing with the situation.

Noting that the Jews were in no hurry to carry out the eviction order, they announced that those who left voluntarily after receiving an eviction order, as a special favor, would be sent to Tarnow which is only a short distance from Cracow, while those who did not comply with the order would be shipped to distant places. The announcement had the desired effect. Thousands of families reported for expulsion.

Our family also gave the announcement serious thought and decided that my brother Pesachyah, his wife and their two children—a three-year-old girl and a two-year-old boy—should report for expulsion, in order to be sent to Tarnow where most of our family lived. This would make it easy for us to stay in touch with them and help them with food and other necessities.

Upon reporting for expulsion, they were taken to an assembly point to join thousands of other families who preferred being transferred to Tarnow to being shipped off to faraway places.

However, as always, the Judenrat, in cooperation with the Germans, double-crossed the Jews. Instead of being sent to nearby Tarnow, they were transported to the Lublin district, one hundred and fifty miles northeast of Cracow where they were released. The Germans knew full well that none of them would be able to return to Cracow without money or special travel permits.

Pesachyah settled his family in Savin, a small village near Lublin. A good-hearted Jew provided them with a separate room in his house, and we regularly sent them food packages. We were pleased that at least he had found a safe haven where he could stay until Hashem would save us from our enemies. At the same time, we held firmly to our decision not to leave the city until we were forced to do so. The longer we could postpone going into exile the better.

At times such as these, there was no shortage of needy families, people who did not know from where their next meal was coming. Seeing their misery, I took it upon myself to raise money for these destitute families. I knew the ideal place for collecting contributions would be the black market on Augustianska Street. Together with my good friend, the well-known communal activist Shmuel Abraham, we made the rounds among the dealers and traders, unaware that the Jewish police had been ordered by the Judenrat to put an end to all black market activities.

One day, as we were collecting donations in the black market area, we were stopped by two Jewish policemen who demanded payment of a fine for violating the law against doing business on the street.

My friend Shmuel paid the fine on the spot, but I refused, arguing that we were not dealers but were only collecting donations. They refused to listen to me and ordered me to come with them to the police station. When I resisted, they called in help to subdue me and paraded me through the neighborhood to the community building which housed the offices of the Judenrat and the Jewish police.

There I was presented to the Chief of Police, a Jew by the name of Patzanover, a known Nazi collaborator. I stood silently as the two arresting officers reported my "crimes." Patzanover's face had a serious expression. Resisting arrest by a Jewish "officer of the law" was no trivial matter. After reflecting for a brief moment, he pronounced his verdict. In view of the seriousness of my offense, I was to be expelled from the city of Cracow. I pleaded, I implored, but it was no use. The expulsion order remained in force.

I was in big trouble, placed under heavy guard until the expulsion order was carried out. As a last resort, I sent a message to my friend Yaakov Yehoshua Korngold, one of the prominent officials in the Cracow community since before the war, informing him of my unhappy situation. He immediately went to Patzanover to intervene on my behalf, and after protracted negotiations, Patzanover agreed to let me go after payment of a fine of fifty *zlotys*, a considerable amount in those days. I borrowed the money from Korngold, paid the fine and was free to go home.

In the meantime, the expulsions were not proceeding rapidly enough to satisfy the Germans. The Judenrat and the Jewish police were not tough enough. The Germans therefore recruited Polish policemen to assist in the expulsion, and these did the job with top efficiency. As a first step, they stopped every Jew in the street to see whether he had a stamped residency permit. Those caught without a permit were shipped off to distant places. Understandably, it became very difficult to venture out into the street.

Once as I was walking down the street, a Polish policeman, who had been hiding in a corner, jumped out in front
of me.

"Let me take a look at your briefcase!" he demanded.

Inside, he found some fresh, warm bread rolls. It was a
serious crime to bake bread or pastries made of white flour,
since this was commandeered to be used by the German
army. I was in trouble.

"Where did you get these rolls?" he asked.

"They're home-baked," I replied instantly. At least that
was not as serious as having a bakery. His Polish brain would
never think of searching my house where he would find a cold
stove.

"If you'll tell me the name of the bakery, I'll let you go,"
he persisted. "If you don't, I'll book you and take you in to the
station."

Of course, I had no intention of revealing to him the
name of the bakery, which belonged to my brother-in-law
Avraham Dershowitz.

He brought me to the police inspector, placing the
briefcase containing the rolls on his desk. I asked him to
return the briefcase to me, but he refused.

I thought that after taking my briefcase, the inspector
would let me off the hook, but he called over two policemen.

"Take him to German headquarters," he snapped.

En route, I asked a passing Jew to tell my family what was
happening to me and not to worry too much. When the
policemen heard me speak to him, they told him to come
along to headquarters, although he had a valid permit.

I don't know what happened to that Jew because we were
placed in separate rooms, but the thought that an innocent
Jew suffered because of me caused me a great deal of

heartache. On the other hand, how could I have assessed the depth of their depravity?

The Germans interrogated me more thoroughly. They insisted that I tell them the name of the bakery where I had bought the rolls. No matter what they'll do, I resolved, I won't reveal the name of the bakery. How can I get other people into trouble? I knew I could be facing the death penalty, but I did not waver.

They wrote a detailed report, frisked me, but found nothing but five *zlotys* which they confiscated. Originally, I had been carrying a substantial amount of money. However, on the way I managed to hide the bills in some small hole. The Germans handed the report to the two Polish policemen who took me with them into a streetcar. Where are they taking me? I wondered anxiously.

After a long ride, we got off at a stop named Lubitch. They ordered me to follow them and led me into an enormous courtyard surrounded by police. In this place, I met hundreds of Jews who told me that this was an *Aussiedlungslager*, an expulsion camp.

"Those being held here," one of them explained, "are people arrested for staying in Cracow without a permit. Everyone receives three meals a day. For breakfast and supper, two hundred grams of bread, for lunch only a plate of soup. There are separate sleeping quarters for men and women. Everyone sleeps on loose straw that is spread on the floor."

"We may be shipped out today," another added, "but no one knows whether we'll be going to Lublin or Tarnow."

Within an hour, to my utter surprise, someone brought me food that had been sent to me from home. I asked how my family had found out my whereabouts so soon. It turned out that one of the salesmen of a company I had been dealing with had observed me being taken into custody. Unknown to me, he also boarded the streetcar and followed me all the way to the compound. I sent a message to my family not to send any more food as I would be shipped out shortly, but I hoped to be back before long with Hashem's help.

The following morning, an SS man entered the hall.

"*Alle manner zur arbeit!*" he bellowed. "All men must go to work!"

I hunkered down behind a pile of boxes and escaped being sent to work. Returning at night, the others told about the backbreaking work they were forced to do and the beatings they had endured. Before anyone had time to relax, another SS man entered.

"Whoever has any kind of money, hand it over to me right now," he announced. "You'll all be x-rayed, and anyone found with money on his person will be sent to Auschwitz forthwith!" By that time, everyone already knew what Auschwitz meant, and the mere mention of the word sent shivers up our spines. But the money remained concealed nevertheless.

As the day progressed, more and more Jews arrived at the compound. In the evening, the people were separated into two groups. According to the Germans, one group was to be shipped to nearby Tarnow, the other to Lublin. I was holding my breath, hoping I would not be assigned to the Lublin transport. We had heard frightening reports about the terrible conditions prevailing there, reports of overcrowding, famine and disease. The unsanitary conditions were said to have sparked an outbreak of typhoid fever among the deportees. Among those felled by the disease was my brother Pesachyah's wife, as we found out later. She was buried in the village of Savin.

Eventually, the Germans ordered everyone into the court-yard where they separated the people into two groups. It was done without a semblance of planning or order, completely at random. "You to Tarnow. You to Lublin."

Fortunately, I was assigned to the Tarnow transport. We were ordered to line up five abreast, in army-style columns. As I stood there, I noticed in the other column an old friend of mine, Pesachyah Kaminker, the *gabbai* of the Zlatopoler Rebbe. He had been shopping when the Germans picked him off the street and put him on the transport. Knowing that he was penniless, I sneaked out of my column to collect some money for him from people I knew and handed it to him.

The aged and infirm were loaded on wagons. All others had to walk under heavy guard to the station, where a number of wagons had been attached to the regularly scheduled train to Tarnow.

The confusion at the station presented the perfect oppor-tunity for escape. However, fearing that others would be made to suffer German retribution I gave up the idea, placing my trust in Hashem to deliver me from their grip.

At eleven o'clock in the evening, we arrived in Tarnow, where we were ordered to wait on the outdoor platform in the bitter cold. Chilled to the bone after a two-hour wait, we were finally allowed to enter the hall of the waiting room. We sat down on the floor under the watchful eyes of our guards, who assured us that by morning we would be set free.

The morning came, but with no change in our status. We heard through the grapevine that the guards were consulting Lublin on whether to transfer us to the Pustkov concentra-tion camp or to release us. Understandably, the mere men-tion of the dreaded Pustkov camp made us quiver with fear.

Meanwhile, the Judenrat, having learned of a group of Jews being held at the station, sent over a large sack full of bread, a container of jam and a large kettle of hot tea. More than anything else, the tea helped revive us, warming our frozen hands and shivering bodies.

Tension mounted with each passing hour. Where were we going to end up? Finally, at eleven o'clock in the morning, the inspector made the announcement.

To our indescribable joy, he said, "All right, you're free to go!"

We all went into town where we were greeted by representatives of the Judenrat who had provided lodging for *Shabbos* with various local families. I myself spent the *Shabbos* at the home of my uncle Shimon Yaakov Friedman.

The first thing I did on entering Tarnow was to send a telegram to my family informing them of my whereabouts, and as early as Sunday morning, my brother Yosef showed up bringing me a travel permit. Not wasting a moment, I returned home to an emotional reunion with my family.

It suddenly dawned on me that the entire painful episode had a bright side. Since my travel permit certified that I had arrived from out-of-town, I was legally a non-resident of Cracow and as such could walk the streets without fear of being grabbed off the street. The decree clearly stated that only residents of Cracow were required to leave town; out-of-towners were permitted to stay. And indeed, whenever I was stopped and asked for my identification this travel permit satisfied the Polish policemen.

Relieved for the time being of the fear of deportation, my thoughts turned to finding ways of earning a living. I traded, bought and sold, taking advantage of every opportunity that came my way, even doing business with German soldiers. But new obstacles arose constantly.

For one, there was the weather. The cold was raw and piercing. A thick blanket of snow covered the highways, bringing traffic to a virtual standstill, throwing German troop and supply movements into total chaos. Of course, it was the Jews who were assigned the job of clearing the roads. But what Jew in his right mind would be willing to work all day in sub-zero weather? The Germans delegated the Judenrat to recruit Jewish laborers, fully confident that these lackeys would find effective ways of handling the problem. The Judenrat would not let them down.

A proclamation was issued stating that anyone volunteering for snow removal would receive one special stamp for each day of work. Those accumulating twelve stamps would receive a residency permit entitling them to remain in the Cracow ghetto. Not surprisingly, a good many people flocked to volunteer for the grueling job.

I was not taken in by their promises.

"Why don't you join the snow removal brigade?" the chief recruitment officer asked me one day.

"I think your promises are nothing but a pack of lies," I replied.

Nevertheless, among the Jews the sole topic of conversation was, "How many stamps did you collect?" Those who had gathered all twelve stamps were congratulated. People thought I was crazy for passing up a wonderful opportunity like this. In the end, they realized they had been the victims of a cruel hoax, for when the deportations began the stamps were not worth the paper on which they were printed.

CHAPTER 2

■

The Yoke of Oppression

WITH THE PASSAGE OF TIME, GOVERNOR-GENERAL Frank recognized that the Jews were not about to leave Cracow voluntarily and that the Judenrat was carrying out the expulsion at a snail's pace. To speed things up he transferred the entire program to the Polish police.

Overnight, the situation worsened. Just going out to buy bread was fraught with danger, since behind every corner there lurked a Polish policeman, ready to pounce on an unsuspecting Jew. We decided the time had come for us to leave Cracow.

Our idea was to relocate to Bochnia. Our plan called for me to load our belongings on a wagon, take it to Bochnia, come back to Cracow to liquidate my business and, finally, to move the entire family to Bochnia by train.

Those who had permits to live in the Cracow ghetto gradually began to move into the ghetto area which was quite small and promised to be heavily overcrowded. Notwithstanding, people preferred moving there to being expelled to a remote location.

The ghetto was intended to house a population of ten thousand, but in actuality, twenty thousand people squeezed into its confines, some by paying bribes to the Judenrat, others by taking up residence without a permit. No one gave any thought to the eventual outcome of this untenable situation.

The deadline for all Jews to be out of Cracow was set for the day after *Purim*, but even well before this target date, most Jews had already left the city. Not everyone departed unscathed. Many people were arrested by Polish police or German patrols as they were making their way out of the city. The argument that they were leaving fell on deaf ears.

Not wanting to place ourselves in jeopardy, we decided to leave at night under cover of darkness, and on the night of *Shushan Purim* we left our home. Sadly, we recalled how in happier years we used to spend this night feasting in the company of family and friends.

A short train ride brought us to Bochnia. As the train pulled into the station we were greeted by an ominous sight. The platform was filled with local policemen checking the passengers' identity papers. Local residents were permitted to proceed, while non-residents were told to line up on the side of the platform. After the usual interrogation, we were led into the waiting room, and when the coast was clear, we sneaked out the back door. With bated breath, we tiptoed through the deserted streets of Bochnia. It was past midnight when we knocked on the door of our cousin Eliyahu Klapholz's apartment, to be welcomed with open arms and a tasty meal. Tired and emotionally drained after the exhausting day, we bedded down in his small apartment as best as we could.

In the morning, our thoughts turned to finding a place to live. This was not an easy task, since the Judenrat, which was in charge of assigning apartments, refused to consider out-of-town applicants. The town was filled to capacity; there simply were no vacant apartments to be had. Since it was Friday we stayed with our cousins for the time being.

On Friday afternoon, after all the preparations for *Shabbos* had been made, a committee representing City Hall suddenly appeared, ordering all of us, my cousin's family included, to vacate the apartment immediately. It turned out that the pastry shop owned by my cousin had been closed down earlier as a result of false charges, and now, as further reprisal, the entire house was to be vacated and sealed. Thus, we all found ourselves helpless, without a roof over our heads, our belongings locked inside the house. But Hashem rescued us. Several hours later, for no apparent reason and without any explanation, the City Hall people returned, unlocked the door and allowed us back into the house to enjoy a truly uplifting *Shabbos*.

Recognizing that finding an apartment was out of the question, we decided to move into my cousin's pastry shop, which was no longer in operation. The pastry shop was located in the basement and consisted of several rooms. A small grated window provided light and air, suggesting a jail-like atmosphere. To us, however, it was a palace. There were eight of us—my wife and I and our little daughter; my mother; my brother Yitzchak and his wife; and my two younger brothers Shimon and Yosef. We settled down, making the best of a difficult situation, but it was not to last.

A few days later, several Judenrat people made their appearance, led by Dr. Rosen, the chief of the Jewish police, a corrupt man with a reputation of being a big fool. Dr. Rosen asked us a number of questions, then he pulled out an official order stating that we had twenty-four hours to leave Bochnia. If we did not comply, we would be forcibly ejected by the German police. We looked at each other, stunned and dumfounded. What were we to do? After many inquiries, we approached a number of channels in an attempt to influence the Judenrat and succeeded in obtaining a residency permit allowing us to stay in our subterranean abode. The next problem we faced was finding a source of income. We placed our trust in Hashem who had helped us until now and would continue to watch over us.

Life under German occupation was extremely difficult but Jewish faith, stamina and ingenuity helped make it somehow bearable.

In every war, the conquering power appropriates all sources of energy, using them for its own war effort. The mines of western Poland produce a rich supply of coal, while eastern Galicia is known for its numerous oil wells. The Germans immediately took possession of these natural resources, creating serious shortages for the local population and for the Jews in particular.

We were forced to improvise. We illuminated our homes with carbide, white crystals that would produce fumes when water was poured over them. These crystals were placed in tin cans, and a thin pipe was inserted through the cover. When the stones were seething, fumes emerged from the pipe which, when lit, illuminated the entire apartment. Occasionally, the can would explode, but generally it was an efficient and inexpensive way of providing light.

Heat was produced by an ingenious method. We would prepare a round tin kettle with a small opening on the side through which we ignited the fire. We would insert damp wood shavings into the kettle which produced comfortable heat, while the smoke escaped through a chimney valve on top. This kettle could also be used to warm up food. But starting the fire took a great deal of skill. If the wood shavings were either too dry or too damp they would not ignite at all. The main problem arose on *Shabbos*. If the kettle was not properly kindled, we could spend the entire *Shabbos* in the cold, eating cold food, and when occasionally the lighting device malfunctioned, we would be forced to sit in the dark as well. At least there was no shortage of wood shavings; for a small amount of money the lumberyard would deliver an entire wagonload of shavings.

Under normal circumstances, our basement would have been unfit to live in, but to us it was a life saver. Each of us found a way to earn a living; my cousin Eliyahu Klapholz taught me to become a pastry chef, which became my new profession. If only we could survive the war years under the present conditions, we mused, things would not be too bad. But it was all just wishful thinking.

On *Chol Hamoed Sukkos* of 1942, the head of the Labor Department turned to the Judenrat demanding a call-up of one thousand laborers to work at the weapons and ammunition supply dump at the outskirts of the village of Klai. As usual, the Judenrat was eager to comply, rounding up all the young men. My brother Yitzchak and I were among the inductees, whereas my brother Yosef managed to elude them. Some jobs entailed very heavy labor, while other jobs were quite easy. People were assigned to do those particular jobs to which they were physically best suited.

We were instructed to appear for work in two days, but the two-day breather gave us little comfort. We dreaded working for the Germans and worried about our lost income. We tried all kinds of intervention, even bribery, but to no avail. We had to swallow the bitter pill and accept our fate.

We rose early to catch the train taking us to work, travelling under the supervision of our foreman, a Jew from Bochnia. The labor camp was located deep in the heart of a forest. It consisted of wooden barracks stocked with various German army weapons and ammunition. It was our job to inspect the crates to determine if the arms had been manufactured according to specifications. Sometimes, we had to move the crates or carry them from one barrack to another, a job that made no sense at all to us. Tracks had been laid over which to move wagons loaded with weapons from one storage shed to another. We started work early in the morning, ending at night, with a break for lunch. Bringing our own food, we had lunch in a separate room, away from the German workmen. At the gate, we were checked by German guards who made certain that all men had come to work. No Poles were drafted for this kind of work for fear that they might commit sabotage—one single match could blow the entire facility to smithereens.

The festivals of *Shemini Atzeres* and *Simchas Torah* were rapidly approaching, days of rejoicing but which we were to spend this year loading crates of guns and ammunition. What should we do on the forthcoming *Yom Tov?* Jeopardize our lives by staying away from work? Aside from evading the German guards, we would also have to deal with the Judenrat, who would probably come down on us even harder. Throwing caution to the winds, we decided to celebrate the *Yom Tov* days in the *bais midrash*, taking part in the joyous festivities.

Apparently, we were not alone in calculating that the Germans would not notice if one lone individual was missing. It brought to mind the story of the two partners who acquired a barrel of wine, each one taking only one little sip for a *lechayim*, thinking the other would not notice it. One drink led to another, until the barrel was empty. In the same way, when *Yom Tov* arrived, there was a large number of absentees, and unknown to us, the foreman complained about the matter to the Germans.

The night of *Simchas Torah* found us in the circle of our family gathered around the festive table, rejoicing, singing *Yom Tov* songs. Suddenly, there was a knock at the door. It could only mean an unwelcome visit by the Jewish police. The two of us slid into the bunker that had been prepared for occasions just like this. Meanwhile, my mother opened the door to the policeman who presented a summons demanding our immediate appearance at the Judenrat office.

"They're not here," my mother said, her voice aquiver.

"If they don't show up, they risk being shot by the labor boss," the policeman replied.

Having no alternative, we emerged from our hiding place and followed the policeman to the Judenrat office. There we encountered a large number of other people who had been arrested, some of them parents, brothers and sisters of workers who had not appeared for work and had gone into hiding. They were being held as hostages to force their relatives to come out of hiding, as indeed they did. Meanwhile, the Judenrat went into session, presided over by Dr. Weiss and Police Commissioner Dr. Rosen.

It was close to noon when the raid was completed, and the labor boss entered.

"Did we catch all of them?" he asked, a cynical smile on his face. His eyes skimmed over the list of names. "Sure enough, they're all accounted for."

Thereupon, he asked each person individually, "Why didn't you show up for work today?"

He received a different excuse from everyone.

"My pants were torn," one fellow claimed.

"My shoes were at the shoemaker's," another ventured.

A third pointed to some injury that prevented him from coming to work.

It did not take long for the German to see through their cover stories. Venting his rage, he slapped and beat the hapless fellows.

"Don't you ever do that again!" he warned them.

Now it was my turn. I had also prepared an excuse which had, in fact, a basis in truth.

"My mother is seriously ill with a case of double pneumonia," I told him, "and I had to stay at home to take care of her."

He tried unsuccessfully to trick me into confessing that I was lying. In any event, he claimed, my excuse was not good enough, since one of us could have stayed at home to take care of her while the other could have come to work.

After whispering to the others, he issued his command. Both of us were to shave our beards and cut our *peyos* immediately—on *Yom Tov*—and go to the labor camp right away. I learned later that, in his view, cutting beards and *peyos* was a more severe punishment than any beating could have been.

The charade continued until at last he let us go.

"You'd better show up for work tomorrow," he warned us, "or else . . ."

My brother and I made up our minds that, in spite of

39

everything, we were going to join the festivities in progress at the *bais midrash*. The thought of cutting our beards and *peyos* on *Yom Tov* never even entered our minds.

Going to the *bais midrash*, we encountered several Jewish policemen who wasted no time informing the Judenrat that the Friedman brothers had the audacity to disobey the order and had not cut their beards and *peyos*.

On the night after *Yom Tov*, there was a knock at the door. "Who's there?" I asked.

"It's me, Horowitz, the Deputy Police Commissioner."

He had been sent by the labor boss to verify if indeed we had not cut our beards and *peyos*.

"I'm taking you in," he said. "The German labor boss will know how to deal with you."

We realized this was serious and that the German might even shoot and kill us on the spot as he had done many times before for lesser infractions. We cut our beards and *peyos*, and we appeared for work regularly every morning.

Working for the Germans was not easy. On the train to work, we were always surrounded by Nazis staring at us with hate-filled eyes. At work, we were constantly in danger of being blown to bits by an explosion, the result of an accident or sabotage. Worst of all, we were forced to work outdoors all day in the numbing winter cold.

Initially, the German overseers did not display any signs of anti-Semitism, but as time went by, they began to show their true colors. A small building within the labor camp was set aside to serve as a prison where one could be locked up for the slightest infraction of the rules. Once I had a taste of this prison for nothing more than being late for work.

Gradually, life in the labor camp was wearing me down. Working conditions became harder by the day, the penetrating cold chilled my bones, and I knew I could not stand the heavy labor much longer. I tried, without success, to find a way of obtaining a release. The work project was run by the SS, and the SS would not dispense with even one Jew.

During the entire period of my work there, in spite of the strict scrutiny of the labor boss, I never appeared for work on Friday and *Shabbos*, because on Friday I would have to travel home after sunset. There was a sizable group of *Shabbos* observers, and the foreman would announce every Friday before leaving work, "Let no one dare take off from work on *Shabbos*. You'll be shot if you do."

In spite of his threat, I stayed home every week on these days, thinking that since all the others heeded the warning and did appear for work, my absence would go unnoticed.

One Friday, the overseer made a speech that had the ring of unusual urgency. He warned us that inasmuch as on Saturday a delegation of top level SS officers was going to make an inspection tour of the facilities, under no circumstances should anyone be absent, no matter what.

I thought I had better not overdo it, and this *Shabbos* I showed up for work. The delegation duly arrived; we could tell by the red insignia on their uniform that they were members of the death squad.

At noon on *Shabbos*, everyone gathered in the dining room for the meal. At the sound of our singing, the German soldiers came to see what was the source of all this happiness. We explained to them that it was our way of celebrating the Sabbath day. They stood there impassively but continued to listen with obvious wonderment.

CHAPTER 3

■

Rescue Plans

PREMYSZLAN IS A TOWN SITUATED IN EASTERN POLAND IN the territory that was occupied by Russia before the start of the German offensive against the Soviet Union. It was there that the Belzer Rebbe fled on the night of *Simchas Torah*, as the German *Wehrmacht* advanced on the town of Belz.

The German *blitzkrieg* against Russia took everyone by complete surprise. It was undertaken in flagrant violation of the solemn treaty signed by Germany's foreign minister Joachim von Ribbentrop and his Soviet counterpart Vyacheslav Molotov. Until the German onslaught, Jewish life in Premyszlan continued in its usual routine. Although the Russians banished thousands of Jews to Siberia, they allowed the Belzer Rebbe to remain, and thousands of *chassidim* continued to flock there every *Yom Tov* to be heartened by the inspiring words of the holy man.

The German invasion of Russia brought an end to all this. The *Wehrmacht* routed the Red Army, driving its shattered forces out of Poland, deep into the heart of the Russian motherland. In the process, Premyszlan was occupied by the Germans. For the Jews, this meant the beginning of a litany of pain and oppression. The local Ukrainians, age-old mortal enemies of the Jews, gleefully joined forces with their German conquerors.

On a bright Friday morning, without any warning, the Ukrainians suddenly attacked the Jewish quarter, unleashing a savage pogrom against the thousands of Jews living there, among whom were counted the elite of Russian Jewry. They began by pillaging Jewish homes and setting scores of buildings on fire, including the *shul* and the *bais midrash*. Not content with this, they ran from house to house, dragging out the inhabitants, throwing them alive into the blazing inferno. Among their victims were the oldest son of the Belzer Rebbe, along with numerous prominent *chassidim* who were cast into the flames of the burning *shul*. It was only through a miracle that the Rebbe's life was saved. The reports of the pogrom plunged the entire Jewish community into deep sorrow and distress.

When I received the sad news, I thought, Who can tell what the future holds? The Ukrainians may organize another pogrom tomorrow. The Rebbe's life is in serious jeopardy; we must get him out of this hell-hole as soon as possible.

Of course, this would not be an easy thing to do. According to German martial law, anyone arriving from occupied Russian territory was considered a communist and summarily executed by hanging. Such executions were the order of the day. A rescue plan would have to wait. However, I made up my mind that as soon as my own situation would allow it, I would move heaven and earth to get the Rebbe out of Premyszlan.

After asking around and questioning many people, I learned that the most suitable haven for the Rebbe would be the hamlet of Vizhnitz (not be confused with the Vizhnitz near the northern border of Romania). Although it was only about five miles from Bochnia, Vizhnitz had not been touched by the war; not a trace of a German soldier could be seen there. Except for the yellow patch that Jews were wearing, life went on as serenely as it had before the war. This was probably because the village had no railroad station and could only be reached by horse-drawn carriage.

I decided to suggest this small town to the Rebbe as a suitable refuge. He could live there in peace and tranquility until, with Hashem's help, the war would end. Or so it seemed to me.

I wrote a letter to the Belzer Rebbe, addressed it to Yechezkel Halberstam, the grandson of the Rebbe of Bochnia, and within a few days, I received the Rebbe's affirmative reply.

Much later, I found out that young Yechezkel had shown my letter to the Rebbe's two closest confidants, Reb Yeshayah Rawer and Reb Yossele Yartchiver, the Rebbe's "ministers of internal and external affairs." Both opposed the plan, thinking that the Rebbe would never leave his family to move to Vizhnitz. Nevertheless, they presented the plan to the Rebbe, and to their surprise, he immediately agreed.

Other *chassidim* were consulted regarding the plan, and a scenario for safely moving the Rebbe was drawn up. Safety was of paramount importance since Premyszlan was in former

Russian-occupied territory. They agreed unanimously that Vizhnitz was the ideal refuge for the Rebbe.

But how was the plan to be implemented?

In Bochnia there lived a Jew by the name of Sala (Shlomo) Grayver, son of Reb Hershel Grayver. Sala Grayver had close connections with the *Wehrmacht* people in Cracow. It should be understood that the *Wehrmacht* comprised the German army, separate and distinct from the SS, sometimes called Gestapo. The SS was the political arm of the German forces, known by the death's head insignia on their caps, which was indicative of their murderous assignment. Grayver had established a workshop in which he employed some two thousand Jews, manufacturing various products for the Germans from raw material taken from Jewish factories confiscated by the Germans. In this way, Grayver had established contacts with the *Wehrmacht*.

My idea was to use Grayver to rescue the Rebbe. I knew that Grayver would often accompany the Germans on their forays into territories formerly held by the Russians to plunder the few remaining Jewish possessions. Could not Grayver be the one to bring the Rebbe out safely as a passenger in his own car?

Being a stranger in Bochnia, I had no personal contact with Grayver. Moreover, the man was a secular Jew who had no concept of what a rabbi meant, much less of what the Belzer Rebbe stood for.

I discussed my predicament with Reb Ben Zion, son-in-law of the Rebbe of Vielipoli, who had had a close relationship with Sala's father Reb Hershel Grayver. I asked him to persuade Sala to go to Premyszlan on his next trip into the former Russian zone and to bring out the Belzer Rebbe as a passenger in his car. Grayver agreed, but at the last minute, he lost heart and changed his mind. A different plan had to be concocted.

Many ingenious ideas were proposed.

"How about sending a Red Cross ambulance with a doctor from Bochnia, ostensibly to transport a seriously ill patient, as a cover for bringing out the Rebbe?"

"But if the border guards would inspect the ambulance, the Rebbe's life would be in grave danger."

"Let's offer a bribe to two German policemen to bring the Rebbe in their police car."

"How can you trust Germans to transport the Rebbe? When they realize their passenger is a prominent Jewish personality, there's no telling what they might do!"

We finally agreed on a plan to hire the Pole who carried the mail every day to bring the Rebbe in his truck. The border guards who knew him well were not likely to stop and search his truck. After a long debate, we agreed to offer him ten thousand *zlotys*. But how were we to raise this huge sum of money? Most Jews had been inducted into labor battalions and did not even have the means to support their own families.

In the Bochnia ghetto there lived a *chassid* of Belz named Moshe Stern, who in the past had outdone himself raising funds on behalf of the Rebbe's institutions. He now wrote letters to all known *chassidim* of Belz, urging them to send financial help to rescue the Rebbe. But although the response was gratifying, we were still far from reaching our goal.

CHAPTER 4

■

Unexpected Visitors

ONE DAY, QUITE UNEXPECTEDLY, WE RECEIVED A VISIT from my brother Pesachyah and his children, a four-year-old daughter and two boys, one a two-year-old, the other a one-year-old baby. We were very happy to see them, but when we inquired about his wife, he told us the sad news that she had fallen victim to typhoid fever and died in Savin, the town to which they had been expelled.

"As a matter of fact," he concluded his sorrowful story, "that is the reason we came to Bochnia."

It was difficult for us to absorb the painful reality; she was the first fatality in our family, a direct result of the German expulsion program. We made room for them in our "apartment"—if that is what one could call our lowly cellar. Even before their arrival, our cellar did not offer too much elbow room, but now we were cramped like sardines in a can.

No sooner had my brother settled down than he began to complain of weakness and pain.

"Just rest up from your trip," we told him, "and you'll feel better."

However, when after a few days his condition did not improve we summoned a doctor who diagnosed him on the spot as suffering from typhoid fever, which he had evidently caught from his wife. The doctor also discovered that one of his children was stricken with the same disease.

The doctor had come during the daytime, and when we returned from work at night, we were shocked to find our house under quarantine, guarded by a Jewish policeman who allowed us to enter. Inside, we learned that Pesachyah and the child had been taken to the hospital and that afterwards the entire house had been decontaminated on doctor's orders. It did not take long for the disease to claim its next victim. My mother, already weakened by pneumonia, caught the dreaded sickness.

Of course, we did all in our power to save her. We arranged for the doctor to visit her twice a day. Day and night, I stayed at her bedside. At first, my wife and my sister-in-law relieved me, but then they too fell ill with the fever. Now the entire responsibility for the household rested on my shoulders; I did the cooking and the cleaning, not to mention taking care of the patients, and in particular my mother whose condition was critical. In spite of that, I did not get tired, nor did I lose hope that they would soon recover.

Finally, my mother reached a crisis which she overcame, and from that moment on, her condition improved from day to day until she made a complete recovery. My brother Pesachyah was sent home from the hospital. His condition improved gradually, but my wife and sister-in-law were still seriously ill.

Reviewing my present condition, I concluded that it offered me the perfect opportunity to be released from work at the Klai labor camp. With that in mind, I approached my foreman asking him to explain to the supervisor that since my household was infected with typhoid fever, and there was a good chance that I would catch it, too, it would be advisable to release me and my brother before we jeopardized the health of the hundreds of laborers. Of course, I promised him a generous reward. A few days later, he showed me our names on the roster of laborers crossed out with red ink, a sign that we were freed from work. I was glad to pay him his reward. Good riddance, I thought, hoping never to see him again.

My joy was dampened, however, when my young daughter was struck down with typhoid fever. Our physician Dr. Lemansdorf recommended that she be hospitalized. Since the nearest hospital with a children's ward was in Cracow, I decided to take her there although I had no travel permit. I was sure the doctor's note with his diagnosis of typhoid fever would get her into the hospital.

Early in the morning, I took her to the station wrapped in heavy blankets, sneaking unnoticed past the Jewish police guards.

Hashem was on my side, for the entire trip to Cracow passed without one German inspection. Getting off at the suburban Prokatzim station rather than at the busy main station, I was forced to walk a distance of several miles, carrying her to the hospital.

But there was still another hurdle to clear. At the gate, I had to obtain a two-day pass admitting me to the ghetto. But what if the guard demanded to see my travel permit? That would be the end of me. I walked back and forth in the bitter cold, unable to make up my mind. At last, I decided to go forward, placing my trust in Hashem.

Entering the gatehouse, I joined the long line of people waiting to obtain a pass. When it was my turn, the guard listened to my story, lifted the cover off the child, took one look at the sick child and gave me my pass.

After having the child admitted to the hospital, I visited my sister-in-law, asking her to look in on the child and keep us informed about her condition.

Now my problem was how to get back to Bochnia without a travel permit. I certainly could not stay in Cracow with an expired pass, and besides, my relatives at home were sick in bed, and I was the only one capable of caring for them. I found myself in a quandary, not knowing what to do. Before I knew it, the two days passed and my pass had expired. Now I was in danger of being arrested as an illegal resident. As if this was not enough, on *Shabbos* morning I woke up with a high fever, feeling a paralyzing weakness in all my limbs. I realized that I could not afford the luxury of staying in bed while my family needed me by their side. All I could think of was finding a way to leave the ghetto and return to Bochnia.

Through a friend who was travelling to Bochnia, I sent a message to my brother Shimon, the only member of the family who was not stricken with typhoid fever, asking him to send me a travel permit as fast as possible.

It was not very difficult to obtain such a permit. A Jew from Bochnia named Yosef Gurgel was involved with certain Poles in Cracow who reproduced permits that were perfect replicas of the German document. These counterfeit permits could be had at the right price, and hundreds of Jews bought them for business use and as an escape ticket in the event of an imminent expulsion *Aktion.*

It was amazing that the Jewish informers never tipped off the Germans about this counterfeit operation. They evidently used it themselves for business purposes, since these travel permits were needed mainly for business travel which involved the illegal trading in foreign currencies. The exchange rates of the various foreign currencies differed substantially from region to region, thus, by buying currencies in one locality and selling them in another, handsome profits could be made. There was vigorous trading in American dollars, British pounds sterling, Austrian gold coins and Russian gold rubles. The money was usually carried in the false bottom of a suitcase, and although many Jews were arrested for a variety of "crimes," the Germans never detected the secret of the false-bottomed suitcases.

My two brothers and I, having no alternative means of earning a living, became involved in this business. Initially, when I arrived in Bochnia, I tried my hand at producing pastry, but my shop was requisitioned by the Germans. There was nothing left for me to do but to turn to black marketeering. Every day, I would travel to Tarnow to visit the main black market. Going there involved great risks, since the Tarnow SS was reputed to be extremely ruthless; no one caught in their net ever escaped alive. More than once, I was stopped and searched by the SS. However, since the false bottom of my suitcase was well-concealed, they only found some personal items, toiletries and some food.

At the Tarnow railroad station, a Polish policeman checked all Jews for travel permits, searching their baggage for contraband and demanding a heavy fine for the slightest infraction of the rules. Because of all these obstacles many Jews tried their best to stay away from Tarnow.

My brother Yossel thought of a clever scheme to bribe this Polish guard. Once, when he was alone in the room with the guard, he approached him.

"Hey, buddy," he said. "Tell me, what nice gift can I get you?"

"I sure could use a nice pair of officer's boots," he replied, giving Yossel a meaningful wink.

Yossel knew it would be difficult to obtain such boots, but at the next opportunity, he brought him a pair of shiny black leather high boots.

"Okay, so who else do you want me to pass without inspection?" the Pole asked with undisguised glee.

Yossel gave him my name and that of another member of our family, and from that day on, he did not give me any more trouble.

As it was, I was waiting impatiently in Cracow for the travel permit, when at last, two days later, Shimon showed up holding the document. Without wasting a minute, I caught the next train to Bochnia. On my way home, I stopped at the hospital and found my relatives much improved. They had been cured of the disease, but due to their overall frail condition, they were forced to stay in the hospital a few days longer. I, on the other hand, felt simply terrible. My temperature was still very high, but I had no time to stay in bed. There was work to be done.

Leaving my daughter in the good care of the hospital staff, I proceeded to Moshe Stern to discuss the fundraising campaign for the rescue of the Belzer Rebbe.

"We'll never reach our goal through a letter-writing campaign," I suggested. "I'll have to call on the *chassidim* in person. There's nothing like a face-to-face talk."

chassid of Belz. Reb Shmuel rushed to the scene along with a doctor to attend to the injured men who were waiting on the highway, while German cars and trucks were whizzing by constantly. It was a miracle they were not arrested.

Having received first aid they continued on their journey to Vizhnitz in a rented car, where they were greeted by *chassidim* whose anxiety had been growing with the passing hours. Their fear turned to gladness when at long last the Rebbe appeared. For a long time afterwards, the Rebbe suffered from the aftereffects of the accident until gradually the pain subsided.

Once, when I visited the Rebbe while he was still in pain, his *gabbai* Reb David introduced me, "This is Chaim Shlomo Friedman, who brought the Rebbe here."

"Yes," responded the Rebbe. "I know, I know."

He offered me a heartfelt *shalom aleichem*, thanking me for my efforts in rescuing him from the valley of death in Premyszlan and expressing the hope that soon we would live to see the salvation of the Jewish people.

After the Rebbe was settled in Vizhnitz, I remained in close contact with his household, making certain that his life was not in danger. Rumors were making the rounds that an *Aktion*, an extermination raid was being planned against the Vizhnitz Jews.

One day, I was summoned to come to see the Rebbe.

"Since I have heard rumors about a forthcoming extermination *Aktion*," the Rebbe told me, "and since the situation is unpredictable, please obtain a travel permit for me. Just in case."

Although he did have genuine Turkish citizenship papers, and foreigners were exempt from anti-Jewish decrees, he did not want to rely on these papers, since during an *Aktion* the Germans would pay scant attention to such documents. They would kill first, ask questions later.

Complying with the Rebbe's request, I procured a travel document for him which was deposited with a reliable *chassid* to be used should the need arise.

In addition to the Turkish papers and the travel documents, we prepared a third escape route. We knew of many instances when people who had legitimate documents were taken to extermination camps or shot to death on the spot during an *Aktion*.

We therefore decided to prepare a bunker where the Rebbe could stay while the *Aktion* was raging, which usually lasted no more than two or three days, and then he would be moved to a safer place.

For seven months, the Rebbe lived in Vizhnitz in tranquility and without fear. When stories began to crop up regarding an imminent *Aktion*, the Rebbe fled to Bochnia where he stayed only one night, because there, too, there was talk of an impending *Aktion*, which did indeed take place a few days later. He then moved to Cracow, staying in the Padgursz ghetto for about five months. When plans for the liquidation of the ghetto were under preparation, he returned to Bochnia. The German commandant of the Bochnia ghetto, SS *Obersturmfuehrer* Mueller, who was aware that the Rebbe was a *Wunderrabbiner*, a miracle-working rabbi, supplied him with an identity card designating him as a tailor, which in effect exempted him from any work. Once on a *Shabbos* morning, Mueller took a notion to call on the Rebbe. They were closeted for more than an hour discussing a variety of subjects. (After the war, Mueller was tried as a war criminal and received a life sentence.) Five months later, the Rebbe escaped from Bochnia, fleeing across the border to Hungary from where he emigrated legally to Eretz Yisrael. Until his dying day, he never left the Holy Land.

I wrote a detailed account of all the events relating to the various phases of the Rebbe's escape. To this day, I have kept the manuscript to myself, and it remains unpublished. During the last year of his life, I visited the Belzer Rebbe in Tel Aviv to ask his permission to publish the memoirs of his miraculous escape. He was adamantly opposed to it. "First, according to Rashi, it is forbidden to publicize personal miracles," he explained, probably a reference to *Melachim II* 4:29. "Second, there are specific incidents in the chain of events I don't want the world to know about. Third, I have my own personal reasons which I cannot reveal." In view of the Rebbe's unequivocal opposition, I decided to abide by his wish, and the manuscript remains with me. I have also rejected the pleadings of certain authors to relate to them certain details about the escape. However, I can reveal a few particulars concerning the Rebbe's escape from Poland to Hungary. I can do so because the Rebbe himself used to recount them annually on the ninth of *Shevat*, amid a circle of *chassidim* celebrating the anniversary of the day he reached the shores of Eretz Yisrael.

In the car driving the Rebbe to Hungary, he was accompanied by his brother, the Rebbe of Bilgoray, and Reb David Shapiro. Also sitting in the car were the driver and the Hungarian officer who helped them cross the border. The entire rescue project was organized by the *chassidim* of Belz in Hungary, under the leadership of Reb Moshe David Hollander (a brother of the well-known Rabbi Avraham Yitzchak Hollander of New York) who labored day and night with selfless dedication. For months on end, he stayed in Budapest, away from his family, single-mindedly working on the rescue effort on behalf of the Belzer Rebbe. It was Hollander who established the connection with the Hungarian officer who undertook the mission of bringing the Rebbe to Hungary, and jointly, they worked out the strategy for bringing it about.

The officer forged a letter written on official Hungarian government stationery, bearing the signatures of high Hungarian ministry officials. The letter to which the photographs of the passengers had been attached read as follows: "The bearers of this document are three Hungarian officers who have been stationed in Warsaw since the close of World War I. At the present time, their presence in Budapest is required so that they can furnish information to the Hungarian Defense Department concerning important military intelligence operations. The Defense Department of the Republic of Hungary requests the cooperation of all authorities in facilitating their journey."

"We had already crossed into Hungary, when suddenly the border guards realized that the three 'Hungarian officers' looked suspicious," the Rebbe would tell his *chassidim.* "They stopped the car, motioning the passengers to step outside. They pulled out their guns, ready to shoot. Believe me, they had every reason to shoot. We certainly did not look like Hungarian officers. I refused to budge, telling my companions also to remain in their seats. The guards kept shouting, 'Get out of the car! Get out! Get out!' No one moved. Suddenly, out of nowhere, there appeared three Hungarian generals riding on horseback, waving the guards away. The startled guards withdrew, and the car continued on its way into the interior of Hungary.

"Who were these three generals? To this day, I don't know. It was a miracle."

The Rebbe then would invite all his *chassidim* to partake of a *seudah*.

Of course, there is much more to tell about things that happened on this trip, as well as before and after. However, in compliance with the Rebbe's wish, I permitted myself to write only the things he himself related.

CHAPTER 6

———■———

Torah and Chessed in Bochnia

DESPITE THE APPALLING LIVING CONDITIONS IN THE Bochnia ghetto and the constant fear that pervaded the atmosphere, the sound of Torah study reverberated through its streets and alleys. There were twenty or so young men who studied Torah without letup in the Sanzer *klaus* (a room dedicated to prayer and study) under the supervision of the young Reb Nechemiah, the son of the *dayan* Rabbi Ben Zion. Although he was barely twenty years old, Reb Nechemiah was chosen to lead the study group in recognition of his proficiency in the Talmud.

Once, while sitting in the *bais midrash*, I was approached by the *dayan* who asked me to undertake the task of underwriting the financial maintenance of the *yeshivah*. He placed me in a dilemma, for what he was asking was no small thing.

People had enough trouble supporting their own families, not to mention the general anxiety about the German expulsions and persecutions. But witnessing the self-sacrifice of the young scholars and their magnificent dedication to Torah study, I was unable to turn him down, and I accepted the responsibility. Until now the students sustained themselves by going door-to-door carrying a basket in which they collected pieces of bread. Sometimes, the *dayan's* children made the collection. I persuaded my friend Rabbi Abba Rosenzweig, an eminent Torah scholar, to take an interest in the students and to arrange exams for them. The *yeshivah* remained in operation until the first expulsion.

I remember an interesting incident from that period. A new SS commandant, a man named Schoenburg, had recently arrived in Bochnia. He was a sixty-year-old German who did not display any particular signs of anti-Semitism and would even, on occasion, do favors for Jews. But he could not be considered a friend of the Jews either, as he eventually showed during the final *Aktion* in Bochnia.

One day, this commandant decided to drop in on the Sanzer *klaus*. The students, seeing him coming down the street, panicked and went into a wild stampede, climbing on chairs and jumping on tables as they tried to escape through the windows. Just at that moment, Schoenburg entered and witnessed the tumultuous scene, the tables crashing under the weight of the students, the window panes shattering.

Thinking he had happened on a secret meeting of a cell of underground revolutionaries, he drew his revolver, aimed at the escaping students and pulled the trigger. But wonder of wonders, the trigger jammed. Much as he tried, it simply would not fire. Meanwhile, the Judenrat was notified, and within seconds, several members appeared to reassure the commandant that the disturbance had been nothing but a group of students frightened by his sudden appearance.

The German accepted the explanation. "You were lucky that my trigger stuck," he commented. "Otherwise, there would have been quite a few casualties." The truth, of course, was that the merit of their Torah study had protected them from certain death.

In addition to the *yeshivah*, there was also an elementary Talmud Torah for small children, headed by the well-known communal leader Reb Mottel Aaron from Cracow, a Torah scholar and a devoted *chassid* of Belz. But with the first expulsion, everything was wiped out.

Although living conditions in Bochnia in western Poland were quite intolerable, they were far worse in the eastern zone which had been under Soviet occupation until the German drive eastward.

This was also true of Premyszlan where the Belzer Rebbe's family and hundreds of his *chassidim* remained after his departure for Vizhnitz. We received countless desperate letters from the Premyszlan Jews telling of grinding poverty and grave food shortages. They pleaded with us to send them food packages, as otherwise they would starve to death, and they included in their letters a list of names to whom the parcels should be sent. The law permitted shipping packages of food and clothing weighing no more than one kilogram (2.2 pounds) from one zone to another.

I immediately organized a drive, and with the money we collected, we bought several large sacks of food supplies. It was not easy to secure the provisions, but thanks to my friend Aussenberg, a *chassid* of Belz, I managed to obtain everything I needed. Being a long-time Bochnia resident, Aussenberg had good connections with some non-Jews who furnished him with any quantity he ordered—charging exorbitant prices, of course. We packaged the supplies in parcels of one kilogram each and sent them to the addresses on the list. Even shipping the parcels required bribing. The parcels were mailed at the ghetto post office, to be transferred to the main post office for delivery to the addressee. Through my friend David Shapiro, we bribed the post office workers to give our parcels preferential handling.

Soon, we received a torrent of requests for parcels, as well as letters from those who had already received them and were at a loss for words to express their sincere gratitude. To them the parcels meant the difference between survival and death. We continued to send such parcels until September, 1942, when the Bochnia ghetto was completely eliminated.

CHAPTER 7

■

Disappearance and Cover Up

FTER THE REBBE'S SUCCESSFUL ESCAPE FROM THE
Bochnia ghetto, we were concerned as to what might
happen to him if Commandant Mueller were to find
out about his disappearance. Since we were not sure whether
the Rebbe had crossed the Hungarian border as yet, we had
to devise a plan to cover up his escape so that the Germans
would not pursue him. As I pondered the problem, I was
struck by a marvelous idea, and without delay I began to put
it into action. I instructed my friend Reuven Walkin to go into
the Rebbe's private chamber, put on the Rebbe's garments as
well as his *tallis* and *tefillin* and sit in the Rebbe's chair. He
followed my instructions, despite his fears that the Germans
might see through the ploy. There simply was no other way
to ensure the success of the Rebbe's escape.

As a matter of fact, a short while after the Rebbe's departure the ghetto was buzzing with rumors. A few people reported that they had recognized him when he boarded a coach early in the morning, leaving for an unknown destination. This was true, for he did travel by coach to Butchkov where the Hungarian officer was waiting for him with his car. Although everything was done in the strictest secrecy, some breaches in security could not be prevented.

The Judenrat and the men of the Jewish police, in an effort to investigate the rumor, sent agents to ascertain whether the Rebbe was in his chamber. Pacing the floor of the waiting room, they tried to steal a quick glance into the Rebbe's chamber. Was he in there?

As usual, the waiting room was filled with *chassidim* who passed the time studying or having a glass of tea. These *chassidim* belonged to the Rebbe's inner circle; yet, even they did not know the secret that the one sitting on the chair was not really the Rebbe. We knew that a secret is safe only if no one, not even the most intimate friend, knows about it. Two young men who served the Rebbe marched back and forth as they always did, and those who dared come close to the door could even hear the voice of the Rebbe, praying and studying. Everything went like clockwork. People who handed the *shamash* their written prayer requests could clearly hear the Rebbe wish them success in all their undertakings. Of course, they were not permitted to enter the chamber, but this had happened many times before.

By now, everyone was convinced—even the Judenrat and the Jewish police—that the Rebbe was still here. After all, there were witnesses who had seen him and heard his voice. Reuven was an accomplished actor, and he impersonated the Rebbe faultlessly.

Driven by curiosity, a larger than usual crowd appeared for the *Minchah-Maariv* service, since the Rebbe always joined the congregation for *Maariv* and *Sefiras Haomer*. But we had anticipated this. The *shamash* announced that the Rebbe was not yet ready to pray, something that was not unusual. The hour of nine was approaching; before long it would be curfew time. Unable to wait any longer, the congregants prayed without the Rebbe and went home. Still, doubt was creeping into everyone's mind. Was the rumor true or false?

The next morning, rumors that the Rebbe had, in fact, escaped from the ghetto were flying again. As we were closeted in the Rebbe's chamber, discussing our plans, we were suddenly warned that the commandant—in the company of the head of the Judenrat Weiss and the chief of the Jewish police Dr. Rosen—were in the building, ostensibly to see if everyone was at work but really to discover if the Rebbe was present. Reuven quickly took off his vestments, and we all made a speedy getaway, leaving just one *shamash*.

The delegation arrived, and the commandant, resplendent in his tight-fitting uniform, went straight into the Rebbe's chamber.

"*Wo ist der Rabbiner?*" he barked at the *shamash*. "Where is the rabbi?"

Without waiting for an answer, he grabbed the young man and took him to the Judenrat building for interrogation. There he gave him a savage beating to make him reveal the Rebbe's whereabouts and the identity of the people who had helped him escape. The *shamash* denied any knowledge.

"All I know is that when I got up this morning, the Rebbe was gone," he stated timidly.

"Who played the part of the *Rabbiner*?" asked the commandant.

"I did."

"But you were outside in the waiting room!" the commandant angrily shot back.

"That's right. Both I and my partner played the part of the rabbi. We received orders from the *Rabbiner* that in case he would disappear, we were to play his part."

The commandant then demanded that the other *shamash* be taken into custody to be questioned. Being assured that no harm would come to him, the *shamash* gave himself up. The commandant kept his word. After administering a sound thrashing, he let both of them go.

For two days, we held our breath, afraid that the commandant might arrest all the people that would frequent the Rebbe's house. We kept a low profile until we were told that the matter had been laid to rest. Subsequently, we learned that covering up the Rebbe's escape proved to be of crucial importance, since the Rebbe needed to remain in Bochnia for two days before setting out on his journey. Discovery of the secret might have imperiled the entire operation.

CHAPTER 8

■

A Helpful Gestapo Chief

STRANGE AS IT MAY SEEM, SCHOENBURG, THE GESTAPO chief in Bochnia, exhibited a surprisingly humane attitude toward Jews. He showed his understanding when he readily affixed the official German government seal to any document declaring the bearer to be a foreign national. Under the German law of occupation, Jewish citizens of a foreign country were exempt from anti-Jewish decrees; included in this exempted category were citizens of occupied countries such as Hungary, Czechoslovakia and Romania.

Understandably, everyone tried to procure citizenship papers or passports of these or other foreign countries. Holders of such documents were free to travel, enabling them to leave the ghetto at the very first rumor of an impending *Aktion*. Unimpeded travel was helpful also for doing business, as the fluctuating currency exchange rates in the various zones presented fabulous opportunities for earning sizable profits.

Additionally, if one held citizenship in a certain country, the members of one's family were automatically considered citizens of that country as well and were exempt of all persecutions.

A person who was not a foreign national would try to obtain from relatives abroad a spurious "document" stating that he was a citizen of a foreign country. He would then take this "document" to Chief of the Gestapo Schoenburg, who would authenticate the "document" by placing the SS seal and his own signature on it. In effect, he thereby exempted the bearer from any harassment and persecution. The news of Schoenburg's good-will spread rapidly, and before long, people from other towns brought him bogus foreign "citizenship papers," and to everyone's surprise, he signed all of them without exception, even though some of them were blatant forgeries.

Although Schoenburg's certifications were very helpful, they sometimes resulted in tragedy. Occasionally, people from Gestapo Headquarters in Cracow would check the validity of these documents and arrest the bearers of fraudulent papers. Furthermore, the Gestapo ruled that all foreign nationals would be placed under its "protection." For that purpose, they were transported to Germany to be interned in the Bergen-Belsen concentration camp where they were interrogated about their vital data and the manner in which they had attained their citizenship. Of course, there were not many who could give satisfactory answers, since most of the papers were illegitimate.

Schoenburg's uncharacteristically benign attitude toward

Jews came to the fore in his frequent visits to the Sanzer *klaus*, the only *shul* in the ghetto. Whenever he had guests, he would bring them to the *klaus*.

No one understood the strange fascination the *klaus* held over him, making him come back again and again. I met him quite a few times when I was sitting outside in the cool hallway, studying regularly every night after coming home from work. Of course, each time I saw him, I jumped from my seat and stood at attention, but with a wave of his hand, he would motion to me to sit down. Although his first appearance in the *klaus* left us all in a rattled frame of mind, his subsequent visits were very congenial.

At a later date, the Gestapo ordered Schoenburg to stop issuing further endorsements of any citizenship papers. They obviously had been swamped with documents of this kind, and they also wanted to stop the steady stream of Jews entering and leaving Gestapo Headquarters to apply for such endorsements.

It was then that Jews turned to forging SS endorsements.

A personal friend of mine, a man named Avraham Mehr, originally from Tarnow, was an outstanding Torah scholar, an enthusiastic *chassid*—and an accomplished counterfeiter. His forged signatures could not be distinguished from the real ones. I urged him a number of times to sneak off to Hungary, but he did not want to give up his lucrative counterfeit business of issuing "endorsements," for which he was paid handsomely. Sad to say, during the last expulsion *Aktion* he disappeared without leaving a trace, along with all the other Jews of Bochnia.

By contrast, there were others who sought to procure genuine citizenship papers. A friend of mine, Nassan Singer from Yaroslav, bought Turkish citizenship for the unheard of sum of twenty thousand *zlotys*. While most of the holders of bogus papers were shot to death by the SS, he and his family passed inspection and were interned in Bergen-Belsen, from where they emigrated to the United States after the end of the war.

CHAPTER 9

---■---

Hazardous Travels

LOOKING BACK AT MY NUMEROUS TRAVELS DURING THAT time, many harrowing experiences come to mind. Once, while on the platform of the Tarnow station I found myself surrounded by several hundred Poles who, like myself, were waiting for the next train. For the most part they were salesmen who were raking in huge profits, taking advantage of the inability of Jews to travel freely.

Just then, an express train was approaching. Since I knew this train would not stop for more than one minute, I elbowed my way through the crowd and jumped on the train, while most of the Poles were left standing on the platform. The train was packed, so that I only found space near the door.

Presently, the German conductor appeared. Spotting me, his face turned red.

"The Poles were left back on the platform, while you, Jew, got on?" he bellowed as he flung open the door. "*Heraus! Heraus!* Get out! Get out!"

My life was hanging by a thread; the German was ready to push me off the speeding train. I said nothing, but I made up my mind that if he tried to throw me off the train I would pull him along with me. Let him be my *kapparah.*

I remained standing there motionless while he continued shrieking, "*Heraus, 'raus!*" Finally relenting, he hurled his parting shot at me, "You'd better get off at the next stop!"

I did not need his order, since the next stop was Bochnia, my final destination.

On another occasion, I happened to be waiting for a train at the Tarnow station. The train, which was scheduled to arrive at seven in the evening, was delayed. I wanted to sit down in the waiting room, but a sign on the door warned, "*Fur Juden ist eintritt verboten.* No admission for Jews." Since I had a long wait ahead of me, I took a risk and entered the waiting room, unobtrusively taking a seat in the corner. The hours went by without incident, but with no train in sight either.

Growing impatient, I went up to the platform where I noticed a freight train pulling in on the Bochnia tracks. It was merely slowing down without coming to a complete halt. Quickly, I jumped on one of the wagons.

Just as I was gaining a foothold on the steps, I heard the voice of a German soldier who must have noticed I was a Jew by the yellow star on my sleeve.

"*Herunter! Herunter!*" he yelled from up above. "Get off! Get off!"

At first, I pretended not to hear him, thinking that as the train gained speed he would leave me alone. But when I saw him point his gun at me, I wasted no time in jumping off the racing train. Thank Heaven, I landed without a scratch.

One day, while travelling from Tarnow to Bochnia on a train crowded with Poles returning from work, I had no choice but to stand on the outside steps. The Poles began to harass me, heckling me with curses and anti-Semitic slogans. None of this bothered me, but when I heard them whisper that when the train passed over the bridge they were going to throw me into the river, I began to worry. The train was drawing nearer and nearer to the bridge; I could see its arching span up ahead. Silently, I prayed to Hashem that He save me. My prayer was answered. The Poles vented their hatred by pelting me with eggs. Jeering and laughing raucously, they savored the pathetic sight of the "dirty *zhid*" . . . while I was delighted merely to be alive.

Once when I was in Tarnow, a fellow I knew asked me to do him a "favor" and deliver a package of old clothes for him. Why not? I was glad do him a favor. On the train, a German inspector came around to examine the passengers' bags and luggage.

"What is in the package?" he asked me.

"Just used clothing," I replied.

He glanced at me suspiciously. "Why don't we have a look?" he said. "If I catch you telling a lie, I'm going to shoot you on the spot."

He pulled out a pocket knife and opened the parcel. I nearly fainted when I saw that wrapped inside the old clothes was a bundle of letters that dealt with black market transactions.

Woe is me, I thought. Now I'm in real trouble. It'll take a major miracle to get me out of this predicament.

However, to my complete surprise, he closed the package

without examining it more closely, and without saying a word, he walked away. Clearly, he had not noticed the incriminating papers. To me, it was plain as day that Hashem had shielded them from the German's eyes.

CHAPTER 10

In Beck's Clutches

T HE PREVAILING ATTITUDE AMONG THE GHETTO POPU-
lation was that in order to remain alive one needed
employment of some sort, that without a "work
assignment card" chances for survival were minimal. The
assumption was that bearers of a work assignment card
would not be deported, while those without a job would be
shipped to "you know where." And so, industrial concerns
producing goods for the German Reich sprung up like
mushrooms, giving employment to thousands of Jews.

In Bochnia, too, an industrial workshop was established,
headed by the aforementioned Sala (Shlomo) Grayver, a man
with close ties to the Germans in general and to the Cracow
Gestapo in particular. Although there were two thousand job
openings in Grayver's shop, it was not easy to get work there.

The Bochnia ghetto held many thousands of Jews, all of them eager to work in Grayver's shop, but the only ones who got jobs in his "factory" were his close acquaintances or those capable of paying a sizable amount of money for the privilege. My family and I also registered for jobs, but I was not about to make any sacrifices in this regard, for I placed very little credence in German promises. I decided to seek a different source of income.

Since it was nearly impossible to earn a livelihood in Bochnia itself, I decided to spend a few hundred *zlotys* on a counterfeit travel permit, which was valid for two months. The Germans honored these specious permits, and I used mine, as I mentioned earlier, to trade in foreign currencies and gold coins. My business took me to Tarnow each day, a dangerous environment where scores of Jews were arrested daily. I was frequently stopped by the police or the SS, but with Hashem's help I always emerged alive.

Aside from the purpose of earning a livelihood, I had another reason for wanting a travel permit. I felt that in case of an impending liquidation *Aktion* I would be able to extricate my family with the help of this permit. I was not sure it would work, but a man must try everything. If it had not been for this I would not have entered into such a hazardous business, for it was as a result of my business that I almost was caught in a killing raid.

Rising one morning in the pre-dawn hours in preparation for my daily trip to Tarnow, I arrived at the railroad station only to find that I had missed the train. I was quite upset, for this was the first time this had happened. But since there was nothing I could do about it I turned back and went to *shul* to *daven Shacharis*. On the way, I encountered clusters of people with worried expressions, huddled in serious conversation.

"Haven't you heard?" one man said in response to my inquiry. "The newly formed mobile killing squads, the so-called *Einsatzgruppen*, have started their deadly operations on a broad scale. They were going from house to house, murdering every Jew they come across. At this very moment, they are on a murderous spree in sixty-five towns and villages in our area."

The news threw everyone into panic. Was our town going to be included in the campaign? Would we be next to be killed? Who could tell? No one knew.

Only then did I fathom the full extent of the miracle that had happened to me when I missed the train. The killings had been concentrated exactly on the route I had meant to travel. Jews had been pulled from the trains and brutally murdered, and the same had happened to the Jews waiting at the stations. However, if a Jew is destined to live, Hashem has many ways to make him survive. With my own eyes, I saw how Hashem in His goodness had granted me the gift of life in a miraculous way.

Meanwhile, our town remained quiet. No one could tell what tomorrow held in store. All we could do was hope for the best. I came home, finding my family deeply troubled, their faces reflecting an ominous premonition.

After breakfast, I went out into the street to hear if there was any news. Hardly had I left the courtyard when a young German hoodlum, about twenty years of age and dressed in civilian clothes, came up to me. He grabbed me roughly by my hand.

"Come along with me!" he snarled.

I was terrified. What was the meaning of this?

He led me back into the courtyard, pulled a gun from his pocket and placed it against my temple.

"Tell me the truth!" he said. "Where is the boy who ran into the house? You showed him how to escape."

I had indeed seen a boy run into one side of the house and out the other, but I had no idea what he was running from.

"I don't know the boy," I replied. "I have no idea where he is."

Angrily, he demanded that I give him the boy's address.

"I don't know where he lives," I replied.

"But you saw which way he was running, didn't you?"

"No, I did not."

He hit me with the butt of his gun, threatening to kill me if I did not tell him the truth. When he finished beating me, he said, "You're under arrest!"

He searched the house without letting me out of his sight. Of course, he did not find the boy who had escaped long before. I wondered who this creature was. Obviously, he was not just an ordinary gunman.

Next, he led me beyond the city limits. Unable to control myself, I asked him where he was taking me.

"You'll soon find out," he replied tersely.

In the distance, I spotted a large building marked *Deutsche Reichspolizei*—German Police Department. This gave me a sense of relief, since I had thought he was taking me outside of town in order to shoot me.

In a special room inside the building, I was again subjected to his interrogation—and another savage beating. I steadfastly maintained that I did not know the boy. Thereupon, he dragged me into the next room to face the police inspector. Seeing that the young thug was not making any headway with me, the inspector looked impatiently at his watch.

"You've got five minutes to come up with the truth," he

said. "If you don't . . ." He let his voice trail off without finishing the sentence, and he merely pointed at the gun lying on the table.

For the next five minutes, the younger German continued whipping, punching and kicking me.

"Well, are you going to tell the truth or not?" the inspector asked me.

"I told you before that I don't know the boy," I replied with feigned indifference. "Go ahead and do whatever you want to do."

The answer was another violent thrashing by the young hoodlum, who ripped my clothes, throwing me like a rag from one corner of the room into the other. Then he took me into the basement and locked me up in a dark cell.

My doom is sealed, I thought to myself.

Barely conscious, I dropped down on the pile of straw, falling into a fitful sleep as agonizing thoughts raced through my mind. Would I ever see the light of day again?

After a while, I heard footsteps coming down the hall. It was the same young Nazi, dressed in a police officer's uniform. This time, he took me back into town to be locked up in solitary confinement in the municipal jail. I surveyed the cell to see if there was a way to escape. The small window was barricaded with heavy steel bars; there was no chance of breaking out. Hunger, thirst, fatigue and pain were taking their toll, but what concerned me most was the thought of the sentence hanging over my head. Engrossed in thought, I paced the floor of my cell, singing in a hushed voice parts of the *tefillos* of *Rosh Hashanah* and *Yom Kippur*, as I reviewed my life—my good deeds and my failings.

The hours went by. Twilight approached and still not a morsel of food, not a drop of water, no one to offer me a word of consolation. Why doesn't my brother Yossel come to me? I couldn't understand it, especially since I knew it was not all that difficult to obtain a release from the German police. There were people with good connections. Couldn't Grayver use his influence to get me out?

It was getting dark, and with it came the cold fingers of despair. But no! I must not give up hope. Hashem can help at any time. I decided that if I was not set free by nine o'clock I would assume that I wouldn't come out of this alive and begin to prepare myself for the end.

The clock in the bell tower of the municipal building rang the hours; the bell sounded nine rings. My life was running out. I sat down on the wooden bench, took a scrap of paper and a pencil I happened to have on me and began writing my last will and testament.

I started by listing the people to whom I owed money and those who owed money to me. Then I formulated the main part of my will, as follows: "I ask my mother, my wife and the other members of my family not to mourn and weep excessively over my passing. We must have faith, believing that everything is Hashem's will. Evidently, in His infinite wisdom He decreed that through my death I redeem the Jews of Bochnia. My older brother Pesachyah should observe my *yahrzeit* and recite the *Kaddish* until my daughter Shaindel will be married, at which time her husband should observe the *yahrzeit*. May you all be blessed with good health and the best of everything."

I lay down on the hard bench, my nerves on edge, imagining at the slightest sound that they were coming to get me. And so the night wore on, a night that seemed endless. Finally, a faint ray of light penetrated the small window. My anxiety began to wane, supplanted by hope. If Hashem has helped me thus far, I thought, then He will surely continue to be at my side.

A few hours later, the door opened and a friend of mine entered. I thought he had come to bid me a last farewell, but to my surprise he told me, "Don't worry, people are working for you, trying to get you out."

He handed me a sandwich he had prepared for his own lunch. He virtually revived me with it, since I had not had a bite to eat for twenty-four hours, and my body was wracked with pain from the beatings I had endured. Yet, I wondered, why hasn't my brother Yossel come to see me? Isn't he concerned about me?

A while later, I received another visitor. This time it was Yossel. Our happiness was indescribable. In a tear-choked voice, he told me that within the hour I would be freed. The good news left me strangely unaffected; after the ordeal, I was emotionally drained. He brought me a sumptuous meal, but I was too excited to eat anything, waiting impatiently for the hoped-for moment of my release.

At long last, towards noon, my cell door opened, and there he was, my nemesis, the German who had arrested me.

"Well, are you going to tell me the truth?" he started again.

I repeated my earlier statement.

"Okay, you're free to go now," he said lamely.

On my way home, people stopped me in the street, staring at me in utter disbelief.

"What happened?" they questioned. "They let you go?"

My release was the talk of town. Wherever I went, people would point at me and whisper, "Look, that's him."

Afterwards, I discovered the real story behind the developments that led to my release. Since just around that time the killing raid by the *Einsatzgruppen* was coming to a climax, the Jews of Bochnia were paralyzed with fear. Even Grayver, the "big wheel," had been afraid to intervene on my behalf, particularly since Officer Beck, the Nazi who arrested me, was involved. It was Beck who had carried out all the executions of prisoners in Bochnia. A rabid Jew-hater, he had been overheard to boast, "To me, killing a Jew is more fun than earning ten thousand *zlotys.*" Only on the following day, after the shootings had died down, did Grayver make an attempt to have me released. The police insisted that the boy who had run away must be handed over to them, but they promised that no harm would come to the boy. When the boy was brought in, Beck slapped his face. Aside from that, all Beck did was fine the boy fifty *zlotys*, which I paid immediately out of my own pocket.

At the same time, I also learned why my brother had not come to see me during my imprisonment. As soon as he heard that I had fallen into Beck's clutches, he tried to enlist the help of people with Nazi connections who could lobby on my behalf, but in light of the ominous situation, no one dared approach the Germans. In desperation, he decided to travel to Vizhnitz to call on the Belzer Rebbe. He told the Rebbe about my arrest and the grave danger I was facing. The Rebbe assured him that I would be released soon.

Towards evening, Yossel returned to Bochnia, where he resumed his efforts on my behalf and did not give up until, with Hashem's help, he succeeded in arranging my release.

At home, my family was overjoyed with my return. They had just about given up hope of ever seeing me again.

CHAPTER 11

―――――――――■―――――――――

The Demise of Tarnow

URING THE SUMMER MONTHS OF 1942, THE SYSTEMATIC extermination program in the towns and villages began to take shape. The Germans followed a well-prepared program. Execution squads, the so-called *Einsatzgruppen*, numbering several hundred German SS and *Wehrmacht* troops, would suddenly descend on a ghetto. While one unit would surround the ghetto with machine guns, ready to shoot any would-be escapee, another unit would charge from house to house, dragging the inhabitants, young and old, into the street. Those unwilling or unable to obey were summarily shot. The Jews were then marched into an open space where they were divided into two groups.

Children, the aged and sick were sent to one side, marked for death. Sometimes, they were shot on the spot. On occasion, they would be hauled in waiting trucks to a nearby forest to be mowed down by machine guns. It all depended on the whim of the German commander.

The able-bodied were ordered to line up in columns, five abreast. Anyone stepping out of line was instantly shot by the guards. Everyone was allowed to take along a minimal quantity of food.

They were then marched to the railroad station to be crammed into waiting boxcars, eighty to one hundred persons to a car. Under these conditions, they would be made to wait several days before the transport got underway. Standing there in the stifling heat, packed like sardines, was simply unbearable. The air was filled with the heart-rending cries of those unfortunate people dying of thirst, particularly the cries of the little children some people managed to smuggle with them in their knapsacks. When the people of the Judenrat tried to relieve their plight by bringing them some water, they were turned back at gunpoint by the Germans. Many died even before the transport started moving.

As the tragic journey continued for several days and nights, many of the hapless deportees, unable to endure the agony, found relief in a merciful death. Every so often, the transport was brought to a halt and the bodies, which had begun to decompose and were giving off an appalling odor, were thrown out.

In the cities and towns, no one had the slightest inkling of where these trains, with their human cargo of thousands of deportees, were going. The Germans made it a point to reassure the remaining Jews that they were being taken to a labor camp to be put to work, but the fact that none of the deportees was ever seen or heard from again belied their story. Nevertheless, as long as we had no proof to the contrary, we tried to console ourselves with the thought that they had indeed been recruited into labor battalions. Only much later did reports begin to seep through about gas chambers and crematoria in which every last one of the Jews was being gassed, in keeping with the program of extermination of the Jews laid out in Hitler's *Mein Kampf*.

When these reports began to surface, some Jews invested a great deal of effort and money in an attempt to learn the fate of the deportees from SS officers, but it was no use. The Germans gave them double-talk, never offering a clear answer.

In Bochnia there lived a certain Eliezer Landau who had ties to the SS commanders in charge of the expulsions in the Cracow district—Colonel Hase, Colonel Heinrich and Colonel Kunde. On one occasion, he asked them point blank whether there was any truth to the stories about the extermination of the Jews.

"We can't give you any guarantees about the fate of children and old folks," they told him, "but all the able-bodied are being sent off to work."

Later on, after a few deportees managed to make a miraculous narrow escape from the hell of Auschwitz, the entire picture was revealed in gruesome detail. This is what they reported:

"For days on end, without letup, transports carrying tens of thousands of Jews from all the German-occupied countries in Europe would arrive—from Poland, Austria, Czechoslovakia, Holland, France and others. The boxcars packed with Jews would be moved on specially constructed railroad tracks into a thick forest where the Jews were greeted with the hellish screams of German guards amidst a rain of clubbing and pistol-whipping to quell any potential opposition from the traumatized victims. Thereupon, they were marched deep into the forest and ordered to undress, and their clothes were examined for hidden jewels and valuables. Naked and barefoot, they were given the command, 'Start running!' The Germans had spread sharp-edged gravel on the path, and after being forced to run for several hours, their feet were a mass of bloody pulp. Those who fell to the ground were shot instantly.

At last, they were led into a 'bath house,' ostensibly to take a bath before going off to work . . . Several hundred people were pushed into the chamber in which shower heads had been installed along the walls. The shower heads were opened, but instead of water, a stream of poison gas emerged, killing everybody by asphyxiation within a few minutes. The bodies were removed through a door on the far side of the gas chamber and taken to the crematoria, while those standing in line in front of the 'bath house' had not the slightest inkling of what had transpired. When the first group was processed, the next one was brought in, and so on and so on, until every last one of the deportees was murdered. There were many extermination camps, and each camp employed a different method. The one thing they had in common was the aim to destroy the Jewish people, an assignment they accomplished with great success."

The only way to escape expulsion, or so people thought, was to be employed in productive work to benefit the German Reich. As the reports of the escapees from the "labor camps" became publicized, there was a mad rush to obtain employment in the industrial workshop in Bochnia, which stood under the management of Grayver, as mentioned earlier. Grayver appointed a special committee to decide who was to be admitted and who rejected. My family and I knew that for people like us there would be no openings in this shop, which only registered people who either had a lot of money or who had close ties to Grayver and his underlings, as was also mentioned earlier. We were disqualified on both counts.

One day, as my brother Yossel and I were walking along the street, we noticed a group of people studying a new list of registered workers that had just been published and posted. Everyone was curious to see if his name appeared in the "Book of Life."

We did not pay any attention to the list. After all, we had only gone through the motions of registering, not expecting to be chosen. To our great surprise, one of the people called me over and showed me that both my name and my brother's name were on the workers list. We considered it a sign from Heaven, and from that day on, we went to work at the plant every day, working from eight in the morning until six in the evening, with a two-hour break for lunch. Still, I did not delude myself into believing that working at Grayver's place was a ticket to survival. On the other hand, I did not want to swim against the current either, all the more so since acquiring the job had been so easy.

This development actually came at a very opportune time for us, because we were no longer able to travel to Tarnow on business. A short time before, while my brother Yossel and I were in Tarnow on business, we were warned that no railway tickets were being sold to Jews, not even to people with special permits. I broke out in a cold sweat; something was amiss. A little later, we heard that all Jews who had appeared at the station wishing to buy tickets had been shot to death at once. Now we understood that a killing *Aktion* was in the offing. In spite of the signs indicating an imminent *Aktion*, there was no panic among the Tarnow Jews. In their innate Jewish optimism, they refused to believe that their days on earth were numbered. Our main concern for the moment was how to sneak out of this impending inferno before it was too late.

Knowing the Nazi tactics, we realized that they were likely to begin surrounding the ghetto at any moment and then our lives would be lost. Going to the station was out of the question, since we would surely be shot. Time was of the essence; every minute counted. Thus, we decided to reach a nearby railroad station and catch the train there.

We hired a horse-drawn carriage to take us to the Mashtzisk station, a few miles west of Tarnow. The driver was delighted to take us, especially since we did not haggle about the fare. We asked him to lower the roof in order to make it appear that the carriage was empty. The driver was surprised that on a hot summer day anyone would want to ride in a closed carriage, but why should he care? It was none of his business. We rode with bated breath until we reached the station. We had to wait for fifteen minutes until the train arrived. With a sinking sensation, we made the familiar train ride, fearful of what might happen, but with Hashem's help, we arrived home safely.

A few days afterwards, people who escaped the massacre reported that during the *Aktion*, immediately after we left the ghetto, several hundred SS and *Wehrmacht* troops surrounded the ghetto. A half hour after we departed, the Mashtzisk station was surrounded and all the Jews trying to escape through there were killed. The killing *Aktion* lasted for three days during which time about ten thousand Jews were murdered. All the streets were filled with the bodies of the victims. About twenty thousand Jews were sent off to the crematoria of the Belzec extermination camp. This was the tragic end of Tarnow, one of the outstanding Jewish communities of Poland. Tarnow had become *Judenrein*, "cleansed of Jews."

CHAPTER 12

■

Preparing for the Worst

WITH GROWING HORROR, WE LISTENED TO THE DAILY reports of the extermination squads relentlessly doing their murderous work in the cities and towns of our region. We realized that, sooner or later, the same fate would befall the Jews of Bochnia. We certainly did not want to rely on the assurances of Sala Grayver, the manager of the industrial plant, who had promised, "As long as I'm alive no harm will come to any of the Jews in the ghetto." He based his pledge on the assumption that the work done by the Jews of the Bochnia ghetto in the factory he headed was essential to the German war effort. But we, that is to say, I and the other people living in our house, were considering a more dependable way of saving our lives. We were thinking of building a bunker, an underground shelter in which we would wait out the storm which was sure to arrive. The plans were drawn up, the necessary preparations made, and since we were pressed for time, we got the work under way without delay.

We went full steam ahead. However, the work could be done only in the late afternoon, since during the day everyone worked and in the quiet of the night the sounds of pounding or scraping would instantly betray our secret.

The site of the bunker was a large room in the cellar of our building. We closed off the cellar door with bricks, coating the outside with a thick layer of dirty plaster to give it a shabby, old appearance, in the hope that no one would be able to tell there had ever been a door.

Beneath the staircase, we cut out a man-size opening through which a person could lower himself into the bunker. Being covered by the staircase, the hole was not discernible. For further protection, we fashioned a board to fit the hole. When the last person had lowered himself into the bunker, he was to place the board into the opening, closing it from the inside and making it virtually invisible. We installed electric lighting, running water, toilet facilities and benches on which to sit or stretch out, all designed to provide adequate shelter for a stay of a few days.

Generally, Jews received advance warning of an impending killing *Aktion* from local people who had connections with the German SS. It was our plan to round up all thirty-five occupants of the house at the first word of an imminent raid, assemble in the bunker and remain there until the coast was clear. The actual preparations were kept tightly under wraps; the more people who knew of our secret the greater the risk of informers and betrayal.

The Germans proceeded with their deportations at a

feverish pace, emptying town after town of the Jewish popu-
lace, until it was Bochnia's turn to suffer the whirlwind of
their evil wrath. Posters appeared on the streets announcing
that the Judenrat was summoning all the Jews of the Bochnia
ghetto to assemble on a certain date at a certain place in the
ghetto. At the appointed time, all members of the Judenrat
were present, as well as the industry boss Grayver. Several
speeches were made, all with the same message: "The fate of
deportation that has befallen our neighboring towns is now
hanging over our heads. There exists, however, one single
route to escape from this disaster. The German authorities
demand payment of a quarter million *zlotys*. In return, they
assure us, there is the possibility that the deportation decree
will be rescinded."

Of course, everyone was ready to part with his last penny
to save his life and the community. The money poured in.
The wealthy gave large sums, the poor gave modest amounts,
and within only a few days, the entire amount—an enormous
fortune in those days—was raised. The Judenrat dutifully
delivered it to the German Gestapo.

It was quite obvious to many people that this was nothing
but a German ploy to extract with ease the last money the
Jews still had in their possession. Thus, there were many who
thought of various ways of escaping, either by excavating
bunkers or by going into hiding with non-Jewish friends
outside the ghetto walls. The second course of action was
nothing more than an impossible dream, since during round-
ups and deportations, the walls of the ghetto were very
heavily guarded. There simply was no way out.

Bochnia was bewildered. Gloom and desperation filled
the hearts of its people. A few more days to live, and then
what? Rumor had it that a special train for the Jews of Bochnia

had pulled into the station. No doubt, our worst fears were about to be realized! There were some who still believed in Grayver's promise. Drowning men grasping at straws! During a raid, the killing of all Jews is sanctioned. The SS makes no distinction between one victim and another. Like mad dogs smelling blood, nothing can stop a German who has been granted permission to murder. There could be no doubt that a raid was in the offing. The feverish preparations around us clearly pointed to it.

We began to make concrete plans to deal with the dangerous situation. The best alternative, we thought, would be to escape from the ghetto. It certainly was preferable to sitting in a bunker. There was only one problem—how to obtain a travel permit. My brother Shimon and his wife, along with my mother and my little daughter Shaindel, had left Bochnia the preceding Friday, since I knew it would be impossible to keep a two-year-old child in a bunker; her slightest whimper might betray the entire bunker population. They travelled to Briegel, a town not far from Bochnia, where we hoped to join them after procuring travel permits to replace our recently expired documents.

To our deep disappointment, the contact arrived from Cracow and told us that no travel permits could be had for all the money in the world. Just now, when we needed the permits to save our lives, it was impossible to obtain them! And we always kept them updated, just for such an occasion. What a terrible tragedy! No, we told ourselves, let's not despair. Let's take heart. *Gam zu letovah*—this too is for the good. Having no alternative, we decided that we—that is to say, myself, my wife, my brother Yossel, my brother Pesachyah and his three children—would remain in the bunker.

Tension and fear pervaded the atmosphere. The entire

ghetto was in an uproar, Jews running in all directions.

"Do you know of a way out?"

"Do you have a good bunker?"

Thoughts such as these were on everyone's mind. Yes, that was to be our *oneg Shabbos*.

Early Friday morning, a long convoy of horse-drawn wagons approached Bochnia from the direction of Vizhnitz. The wagons were loaded with Jews—men, women, children, old and sick people—and their meager possessions. They were coming to settle, of all places, in the Bochnia ghetto. A few days earlier, they had received instructions to move to Bochnia before *Shabbos*, where they were to be housed in apartments. Similar instructions had been issued to the Jews of the other towns in the Bochnia district, and now they were all flocking to Bochnia in one mass influx.

The wagons clogged the narrow streets, creating sheer pandemonium, and were directed to the railroad station by Polish policemen. There, the people were put up in large barracks where they would stay—so they were told—until adequate housing could be prepared for them.

It dawned on a few people that they were the victims of a cruel German hoax. Realizing that they were being led like sheep to slaughter, they jumped off the wagons, oblivious to the guards surrounding the convoy. They knew that by jumping off the wagons they had nothing to lose. The "jumpers" quickly blended into the ghetto crowds, finding shelter with relatives and friends. I myself saved a number of my acquaintances on the wagons, signaling to them that they had better jump while they still had the opportunity. As a result of admitting these refugees, however, our bunker became very overcrowded. Still, we felt it was our moral duty to help these people as they were in far greater peril than we were. At that time, we still lived under the illusion that the Germans were interested only in deporting the Jews of the surrounding area. We still believed that Bochnia would be spared, for hadn't Grayver given us his word?

On *Shabbos* morning, our bunker was filled far beyond capacity. We had designed it to house thirty-five occupants, and now it held one hundred fifty persons! The air was stifling, the heat unbearably oppressive. Moreover, because of the many refugees, the existence of the bunker became known throughout the ghetto. The secret was out, thus it no longer made sense to hide in the bunker.

After pondering the problem, I decided not to use the bunker. In the wake of the publicity our bunker had received, its eventual discovery was a foregone conclusion. Besides, as a result of the overcrowding, one could not possibly stay there for more than a few days at the most. A new bunker had to be found.

Time was running out. The atmosphere was tense, charged with anxiety. I recalled that our *mechutan* had prepared a bunker for his family. We approached him, but after taking one look at his bunker, we realized that it would be impossible for us to stay there. It was far too small; there was barely enough space to accomodate his own family.

The final hour was approaching rapidly. We had no choice. We had to find a solution. We decided to divide the family into two groups. Pesachyah and his three children would remain in the large bunker. There were other children there already, so a few additional youngsters would make no difference. On the other hand, the bunker of our *mechutan* held adults only. We squeezed my wife and my sister-in-law (my brother Yitzchak's wife) into it. For my brother Yossel and me there was no alternative but to leave town. To be sure, we had no travel permits, but seeing no other way out, we placed our faith in *Hashem Yisbarach* and decided to head for Briegel.

Happily, we had no reason at all to be concerned about our brother Yitzchak. As we saw it, he was fortunate enough to be in a location where he was fully protected. Two weeks earlier, while working at his job in the carpentry shop of the German labor battalion, his hand had gotten caught in the power saw, and two of his fingers were badly mangled. He was taken to a hospital outside the ghetto where the two fingers were amputated. Subsequently, he developed various complications requiring further surgery. The state of his general health deteriorated markedly, something we considered a stroke of luck, as until that time the Germans had never harmed hospitalized patients. As a matter of fact, Jews were known to pay considerable sums of money to be admitted to a Jewish hospital. Consequently, we did not worry about Yitzchak at all. He was certain to survive.

For a few days, the kitchen of our house was astir as though there were a wedding just ahead. The baking and cooking were in full swing to prepare the food for the days the family would be underground until the *Einsatzgruppen* squad left town. We hid our clothes away in a safe place, where the Germans would not find them. After all, we hoped to come back and use the clothes again.

The time had arrived to put our plan into action. There was no more time for daydreaming, no more time for wishful thinking. At any moment, the Germans were likely to come and surround the ghetto, and then we'd be trapped. With a heavy heart, my wife consented to our parting. She understood all too well that, sadly, this was what had to be done under the present circumstances. I handed her a large amount of money should the need ever arise to ransom herself. Silently, we looked into each other's eyes. She wept bitterly, as though deep in her heart she knew we would never see each other again.

CHAPTER 13

∎

Bochnia Besieged

THREE OF US HEADED FOR BRIEGEL, MY BROTHER YOSSEL, our friend Reuven Walkin and I. We did not know exactly how to get there and were afraid to use the highway which was patrolled by the SS. We were forced to walk through the fields in the general direction of Briegel.

We were about a mile and a half outside Bochnia when we noticed a German cyclist gaining on us. He was one of the so-called *Volksdeutsche*, Polish citizens of German extraction, who were recruited as auxiliaries to the German police force and who enthusiastically participated in all persecutions. In his black uniform, he was a fearsome sight. He stopped us, asking to see our papers. When we showed him our identification documents, he confiscated them and put them in his pocket.

"Where are you heading?" he demanded.

Ordinarily, we didn't frighten easily, but this question scared the life out of us. We realized at once its dangerous implication.

"Both of my children disappeared this morning," I told him, looking him straight in the eye. "Some people saw them walk off in this direction, so we're trying to track them down." To give my answer added credibility, I continued, "Won't you please help us find them? You can ride ahead of us, and we will follow you."

"First, you'll come with me into town," he replied. "There we'll look into the matter."

Things looked bad. We would actually be walking straight into the lion's den. Before we left Bochnia, we had heard of several cases where Jews walking in the street had been shot to death, and surely now that we had been caught in the act of committing the serious crime of leaving the ghetto we were doomed. We pleaded with him to give us back our important papers, mainly the worker's certificate which the Germans respected to a degree, but he insisted that we come along with him. Meanwhile, he entered a village, inspecting all the farmsteads to see if there were any Jews hiding out. And we followed him, urging him to return our documents, but he callously turned down our requests and insisted on taking us in. We had our backs to the wall. How could we break loose?

While he made his search in the village, we made plans to save our lives. I suggested we ask once more for our papers, and if he still refused, we would have to get rough. "Why should we lose our young lives?" I exclaimed. "Instead, let's finish him off, and that will be the end of that."

The others were shocked at my suggestion, looking at me with wide-open eyes, as if to say, "What? Kill a man? Since when does a Jew use the tactics of Esav?"

I repeated to them the saying of our Sages, "If someone wants to kill you, be quick and kill him first." Since going back to the ghetto meant certain death for us, it was our obligation to fulfill this command.

They reluctantly agreed. However, they insisted that I first make a final attempt to plead with him. I decided to propose a deal.

"How much is it worth to you to let us go?" I asked.

The German was confused, and after brooding over it for a while, he said, "I want three hundred *zlotys*."

It was a substantial amount, but without hesitating, I took out the money and pressed it into his hand. Thanking us for the money, he returned the papers and accompanied us part of the way, giving us directions to Briegel. On the way, he caught another prize. He found a Jewish woman, whom we did not know, hiding out in the tall grass. We quickly came to her help, negotiating with him for her release, and for an additional fifty *zlotys*, he let her go and went on his way.

Having benefitted from one miracle, we now needed another miracle. We were about to enter the town of Briegel, the home of a German policeman named Lapsch who was known to grab every Jew who crossed his path and shoot him to death without compunction. We could only hope and pray to Hashem that He would protect us from falling into this monster's hands.

Plodding through fields and forests, blundering about without food or drink, the sun beating down on us mercilessly, we finally reached the town of Briegel. It was *Shabbos*, but there was not one Jew to be seen in the street. Arriving in the Jewish quarter, we were surprised to find it fenced in with wooden boards; as far as we knew the Jews of Briegel had not been confined to a ghetto. We entered through a crack in the fence, happy to have eluded the Germans.

Shabbos afternoon, towards twilight, the cooler air brought people out into the ghetto streets for a refreshing walk, as if nothing had happened. These people have no idea of what has occurred just a short distance away, I thought.

Our arrival created quite a commotion; scores of people surrounded us, bombarding us with questions about events in Bochnia. Our relatives were happy to see us, but on the other hand, everyone was beset with worry about the fate of loved ones in Bochnia. After hearing our reports, the Judenrat people tried to get in touch with Bochnia. No response, nothing at all.

We knew this was an ominous sign. The worst was undoubtedly happening. After several unbearably anxious days, a messenger brought a letter from Pesachyah telling us that at least he and his three children had survived the massacre, notwithstanding that they had been hiding in an "unsafe" bunker. On the other hand, my wife and my brother Yitzchak's wife had been caught and shipped off on a transport. The report plunged us into bitter grief. We knew with certainty that we would never see them again.

The murderous *Aktion* had subsided, and we began to think about returning to Bochnia. My brother Yossel and I rented a carriage and returned safely. That we were not stopped even once en route was in itself a miracle.

Entering Bochnia, we were greeted by a sight so infernally hideous and appalling as to defy description. The streets were deserted, the few remaining Jews walked about in a daze, their parents and relatives having been shot dead in front of their eyes, the others sent to the Auschwitz gas chambers. The house where I lived presented a scene of unspeakable horror. The building looked like a slaughter-house. The walls splattered with the blood of our martyred ones bore silent witness to the carnage. Whoever had been found in the bunker was shot to death, every last one.

"These bloodstains will never be wiped away," I said to myself, "until the day the Almighty avenges the blood of the innocent victims of these vile murderers."

I was told that the Germans had rounded up all the rabbis of the ghetto into one courtyard, made them lie on the ground and taunted and ridiculed them for a long time before cutting them to ribbons with their machine guns. Dozens of torn *talleisim* and ripped garments littered the streets. We went home, but horror of horrors, we found the doors smashed and total wrack and ruin inside. We went down into our basement apartment.

Eerie silence. Not a soul. Nobody, nothing. Emptiness and desolation. They've all been gassed, I thought. Gone up in smoke.

Next, we went to the hospital to see our brother Yitzchak, taking some food with us. Entering the room where his bed used to be, our hearts stood still.

"Where is my brother?" I asked.

Instead of answering, the other patients directed us to the office. "You'll find out from them."

Sadly, we were told that he was not alive anymore. During the *Aktion*, a company of Jewish police came with wagons onto which they loaded all Jewish patients, ostensibly to transfer them to the Jewish hospital. They were, in fact, brought to a number of waiting trucks into which they were flung like sacks of potatoes and taken to the village of Botchkov. On arrival, they were shot dead and thrown into a pit that had been dug for this purpose, many of them buried while still alive. At the same time, scores of elderly people, women and children were mowed down in the same manner. Twelve hundred Jews, my brother Yitzchak among them, as well as my uncle and cousin, are buried in this mass grave. My cousin had received a SS permit to remain in the ghetto, but when he came to accompany his father, he, too, was grabbed and killed.

Our pain was too great to bear, but we decided not to disclose everything to our mother, who had returned from Briegel. What she did know was more than enough. Our family had paid a heavy price in the *Aktion*, but we encouraged each other to accept this Heavenly decree with love. A Jew must find strength in his faith and believe that at least those who escaped the flames would survive the war. Unable to bear the thought of staying in the basement, whose walls reminded us of our dear ones who were no more, we moved into a different apartment. There was no longer a shortage of apartments; of eight thousand Jews only seven hundred remained alive. Nevertheless, the Judenrat took the opportunity to cause us a great deal of trouble for moving without their permission. We settled the matter by paying them off. Life began to take on a semblance of normalcy when we took into our household a little orphan, a nephew of mine whose mother had brought him to Briegel and whose parents had both been shot to death.

We wanted to out find why all the occupants of our bunker had gone voluntarily to the deportation train in spite of our warning that under no circumstances should they do this, not even under the threat of death. We had explained to them that the trains would take them to the gas chambers to suffer a slow and agonizing death. After making inquiries, we learned that they had been tricked by the Jewish police who had announced, "Anyone coming to the train voluntarily will only be sent to a labor camp. Anyone caught afterwards will be executed." Many people fell for this ruse, preferring to be shipped off to work, as long as they would stay alive. They could have saved themselves if they had not been seduced by this promise. Indeed, those who remained steadfast were saved and stayed alive.

The Germans themselves did not believe that it would take only three days for them to empty the ghetto. They had the Judenrat to thank for their faithful service. The feelings of the Judenrat people had become dulled to such an extent that they did not hesitate personally to bring to the death train their own parents and family members. With respect to assisting the Germans, the Judenrat members of the Bochnia ghetto outperformed all other ghettos. It was only after the *Aktion* had ended that some of the members realized the enormity of their crime. By then it was too late; the smoke of the burning Jewish bodies was already rising from the smokestacks of Auschwitz.

Difficult though it may be, we realized that we had to attempt to banish from our thoughts the overwhelming pain of the past. The German killers had not yet laid down their arms, and we had to find ways and means of staying alive. Employment in Grayver's plant was no insurance for survival. I and a few other workers were still licensed by the Gestapo, but the majority had been deported along with everyone else.

Sala Grayver met the same tragic death as the Jews whom he meant to shelter under his protection. On the very first day of the *Aktion*, he was shot to death by the SS. He did enjoy the respect of the *Wehrmacht* people in Cracow, but the SS held him in contempt. (A deep hatred divided these two branches of the German armed forces, and generally, the SS, being the political branch, held the upper hand. The SS, taking advantage of every opportunity to humiliate its rival, was delighted to dispose of the *Wehrmacht's* Jewish protege Grayver.)

The German Chief of Labor in Bochnia was an SS man, but Grayver paid scant attention to him. He relied on the fact that he employed in his industrial plant two thousand Jews producing goods for the *Wehrmacht,* whereas the SS was not concerned with industrial production at all. While the *Aktion* was raging, and ninety percent of the Jews of the Bochnia ghetto were being deported to Auschwitz, the Chief of Labor leveled a series of false charges against Grayver. The *Wehrmacht* was unable to protect him, because during an *Aktion* everything is under SS control. The Chief of Labor arrested Grayver, beating him to a pulp and, according to some reports, finally drowning him. People had warned Grayver to go into hiding during the *Aktion,* as the Labor Chief undoubtedly would want to get even with him, but Grayver was too arrogant to take the advice. In the final analysis, it was his haughtiness that led to his tragic downfall. Grayver failed to understand that in spite of his prestigious position he was still a *Jude,* and when the chips were down, he was no different from any other Jew.

CHAPTER 14

■

The Rakowitz Labor Camp

ONE DAY, MY MOTHER, YOSSEL AND I WERE GATHERED around the table for lunch when two Jewish policemen, Shomo and Yoske Greiber, suddenly entered, and demanded to see our papers. I got up and showed them my worker's permit.

"Okay, that's fine," they said.

Yossel, however, had no such permit, and the policemen insisted that he come along with them to the station. I knew right away that there was trouble afoot; there was probably another *Aktion* brewing.

Yossel pleaded with them at least to allow him to finish lunch. They agreed to wait for him, but since the room was very crowded they went out into the hall. Of course, Yossel's mind was not at all on his meal. He was looking for a way to

107

escape, and when he saw that the coast was clear, he sneaked out through the courtyard, making a quick getaway. The policemen, wondering why it was taking us so long to finish the meal, came back in and were taken aback to see that Yossel had eluded them.

"Where did he go?" they shouted at me, livid with rage.

"How should I know?" I shot back. "It was your job to watch him."

"If that's the game you want to play," retorted Shlomo Greiber, "we'll take you in instead of your brother."

"Oh no, I won't go. You won't use me to cover up your mistake. And besides, you have no right to arrest me. I hold an official worker's permit."

He grabbed for me, and I shoved him. He punched me, and I struck him. We were getting into an all-out fist fight until he reached for his rubber nightstick and savagely beat me over the head with it. Still, I refused to go. Knowing the callousness of Dr. Rosen, the head of the Jewish police, and Simchah Weiss, the boss of the Judenrat, I was convinced that at the Judenrat I would not stand a chance, in spite of my worker's permit.

In the aftermath of the brawl, a crowd gathered in front of our house. Several policemen burst into the apartment to help their beleaguered comrades. With all my strength, I tried to resist them, but realizing I was fighting a losing battle, I gave up and was taken to the Judenrat building. After listening to Greiber's report, all members decided unanimously that I should be held in custody in my brother's place. Hoping to change their mind, I pulled out my worker's permit, but Horowitz, the Deputy Chief of Police, tore it into shreds and slapped my face for having the audacity to speak up.

Next, I was locked up in the basement jail where I met a large number of other Jews who had been arrested, waiting to be shipped to a labor camp. On orders of the Germans, one hundred workers had to be recruited, and with new men joining us in the cell constantly, it was not long before the quota was filled.

Toward evening, we were taken to the large hall of the Judenrat building where we spent the night sitting on the floor, trying to doze off. I surveyed the scene, looking for a way to escape, but we were guarded so heavily that I quickly abandoned any such thoughts. At the same time, I still kept hoping that my worker's permit would get me off, thinking that it would be an insult to the German Labor Department if one of their licensed workers had been arrested. My mother asked the plant manager to intervene on my behalf, but Simchah Weiss could not be dissuaded.

In the morning, we were made to line up in the courtyard, while the Judenrat people gleefully watched their catch. The German inspector, a notorious Jew-hater, checked off the prisoners list.

"*Alles in ordnung*," he said, with a sadistic smile. "Everything is in order."

Now we were waiting for the trucks to take us to work. But to which camp?

"To the labor camp near Plashow," we were told. "Not far from Cracow."

The name Plashow did not alarm me, since as far as I knew this camp was not kept under heavy guard. I had heard that on occasion the workers would be brought to the Cracow ghetto to take a bath, and once in the ghetto, I would do my best to stay there. The way I figured it, being sent to Plashow could turn out to be a blessing in disguise, since I had meant to spend *Sukkos* with the Belzer Rebbe in Cracow. It looked as if everything would work out just according to plan. The truck would take me to Plashow, and from there it would be only fifteen minutes to the ghetto and the Belzer Rebbe. I had been preparing for my escape even while I was still in the basement jail of the Judenrat, pasting together the torn pieces of my worker's permit until I again had a valid identification document.

It was noon, the day before *Sukkos*. Two trucks guarded by Jewish policemen were waiting to transport us to our destination. Under the eagle-eyed supervision of the SS camp commandant, we boarded the trucks while each of us received three cigarettes and a piece of dark bread in honor of *Yom Tov*, courtesy of the Judenrat. Now we were told that instead of Plashow we were going to an airfield at the outskirts of Rakowitz, which is also not far from Cracow. I was unfamiliar with the conditions of this camp. Well, I'll probably be able to escape from that camp, too, I thought to myself.

The convoy began to move. People waved good-bye, wishing us a speedy return. Passing through my street, I saw people lining the sidewalk, calling out their good wishes. My mother was standing in front of our house wringing her hands in despair; this was not the kind of *Yom Tov* she had expected. The horrors of the recent past were still fresh in her mind, and now this. Who knew if she would ever see me alive again? The mere mention of the hideous word *lager* (camp) was enough to evoke shudders of terror and anguish.

I tried to cheer her up by calling out, "Don't worry, Mother. I'll be back very soon!" As an additional sign of my confidence I tossed my food ration over to her. "I won't need this any longer," I shouted. "I'll be in Cracow for *Yom Tov*, and there I'll have all the food I want."

The other prisoners looked at me with raised eyebrows. What is he so happy about? Where does he get his self-assurance? Their skeptical looks did not faze me. I firmly believed I would not work in this camp and that before long I would be back home.

After an hour's ride, the gate of the camp emerged in the distance. The truck came to a halt to pass German inspection. The driver shows his documents. Everything was in order. No problems.

The gates opened wide, and we found ourselves inside the camp. Looking around, I noticed that the camp was surrounded by a barbed wire fence. Not exactly what I had expected, it was a heavily guarded military airfield. Even before getting off the truck I realized that my only hope for escape was to take advantage of the procedure whereby all newly arrived workers were driven to the ghetto to take a bath.

After a short ride through the camp, the truck stopped on a large field where we were told to get off. A group of German engineers was waiting to screen the new slave laborers. The work to be done included construction, sewerage, building a concrete runway and other hard labor jobs. The engineers assigned the various jobs according to physical strength. Everyone tried to be designated to the toughest work, since the prevalent thinking was that those working at easier jobs would be killed off. I followed the rule I had set for myself never to volunteer for any work; whatever will be, will be.

This time my policy proved to be right. Those doing the hard jobs suffered gravely. Doing their backbreaking work, they received endless lashings and clubbings, and when they asked to be transferred to lighter jobs, it could not be done.

At noon, the current workers showed up for lunch which consisted of soup that looked more like pieces of garbage floating in muddy water. The Germans told us that we were not really entitled to this food because we had not done any work, but out of the goodness of their hearts, they would let us have some soup. Just looking at it was enough to make you throw up.

Having received this gracious welcome, we were curious to see what our lodgings would be like. After supper, we joined the other workers on their way to the barracks, *davening Minchah* as we marched. Among the marchers, I met a number of friends who brought me up to date on the conditions of the camp. But why should I care? I did not intend to stay here for more than a couple of days at the most!

As we marched, I focused on the activities going on around me, the deafening noise of the planes taking off and landing, the flashing red guiding lights all along the runway.

"This is where we sleep," the other workers told us.

Entering the barbed wire enclosure, we were counted by a German guard.

"Who lives in the small barracks over there in the back?" I asked.

"This is for the camp police," I was told. "Poles in black uniforms whose job it is to keep order and prevent anyone from escaping. They give you the treatment for the slightest infraction of the rules."

Our barracks, which used to be a cattle barn, had a concrete floor and small steel barred windows spaced far apart. The air was stifling. There was no electric light; it was pitch-dark. Someone produced a small petroleum lamp that produced enough light for me to discern our sleeping accomodations. All along the floor of the barracks, arranged in four straight rows, there were burlap bags filled with wood shavings. Between the rows there was space for people to pass. There were no blankets; you used your clothes for covers and pillows. After sleeping on the hills and valleys of these mattresses, everyone woke up with a backache.

In spite of everything, I did not forget that tonight was *Yom Tov*, and neither did the many other religious prisoners. We numbered several *minyanim* as we proceeded to *daven* the *Maariv* of *Yom Tov*, each one of us pouring out his heart through the words of the prayer, sung to the familiar festive melody with mournful undertones. In our thoughts, we relived the past. We saw ourselves going to the brightly lit *shul* wearing our festive garments. We heard the *chazzan* intone the ancient chants that would elevate us into a higher world. We saw our homes, how they sparkled with cleanliness, as the fragrant aroma of the delectable *Yom Tov* dishes emanated from the kitchen. In our mind's eye, we entered the beautiful *sukkah*, its walls adorned with decorative paintings and artistic designs, the *sechach* festooned with fruits and colorful paper chains. We could see the entire family gathered around the *Yom Tov* table, set with ornate china and silverware, as the warm sounds of the harmonious *Yom Tov niggunim* resounded throughout the neighborhood. Ah, the true spiritual joy of *Yom Tov*!

Tears blurred my eyes, and my heart suffered in silence. Gone was all this glory, vanished into oblivion. Here it is *Sukkos*, and I am praying in the black darkness of the German hell—a world where *Yom Tov* does not exist, where joy is banished. Smiling through our tears, we encouraged each other.

"Keep your chin up!"

"Hashem will help us."

"Everything will turn out all right"

"Soon we'll celebrate *Shabbos* and *Yom Tov* again, just as we did before."

"No, even better than before!"

"Take heart!"

"Hang in there!"

We made *Kiddush* over the piece of dark bread, which also served as our *Yom Tov* meal; sadly, the *berachah* over the *sukkah* was omitted. With broken hearts, we sat down on the floor to eat the dark bread and wash it down with a cup of water. This concluded the meal.

Before going to sleep, we continued to comfort each other, but as we were talking, a guard appeared.

"Everybody in bed in five minutes!" he shouted.

It was nine o'clock in the evening, and at five in the morning, we had to get up for work. Everyone found his mattress and lay down. Unable to find a vessel to use for hand-washing in the morning, we filled a few bottles with water and lay down to sleep.

Tired and exhausted, I fell into a deep sleep, but before I knew it I heard the wake-up call, "Time to get up!"

I did not feel like getting up. It was *Yom Tov* today. But there was no time for memories. The Jewish policemen were hounding us.

"Get up, get up," they yelled. "*Schnell, schnell.* Hurry up! Hurry up!"

We washed our hands with the water in the bottles we had prepared and tried to catch a hasty *Yom Tov Shacharis*, but before we could end the service, the black uniformed Polish guards burst in, clubbing indiscriminately with their truncheons, left and right, on the head, the shoulder or any part of the body. Throwing off our *talleisim, siddurim* still in hand, we ran out to the *appell*, the roll call. We were told to line up in column formations of five abreast. Then we were marched to the gate, where we were counted like cattle before proceeding to work.

The gates opened wide, and after a half-hour march under the watchful eyes of Jewish guards, we arrived at the work site. Everyone received his tools, and the work began. We dug, chopped, shovelled and scraped, while our minds were filled with the thought that it was *Yom Tov* and we were desecrating the holy day!

After a few hours of work, we received some black coffee; this was our breakfast. And by the time the coffee arrived from the kitchen, it was already cold.

At twelve o'clock, we had an hour-long lunch break. The religious Jews decided to remain at the work site and use the hour to complete the prayers. We recited the *Hallel* with loud voices but bleeding hearts, mindful that we were at the mercy of our oppressors who could do with us as they pleased. We prayed out in the open, but when we noticed a German approaching in the distance, we went into the pit we had just dug and completed our prayers there. The *Yom Tov* meal was no different from the previous day's meal—a slice of dry bread and water.

Returning from work in the evening, we *davened* and ate again, and this is how we spent the *Yom Tov*, without a *sukkah*, without a *lulav*, without an *esrog*. But *baruch Hashem*, we made it through the day.

My plan of escaping on the way to the bathhouse in the Cracow ghetto had to be shelved, because we were never taken there. Thinking of an alternative, I dreamed up what I thought was a clever scheme. It was camp policy that prisoners who were not feeling well were directed to the Jewish camp doctor. If he found them to be seriously ill he turned them over to Jewish policemen for transfer to the German Medical Director of the camp. If the Director concluded that the patient required hospitalization, he would issue a transfer card whereupon the Jewish police would take him to the local hospital. I picked a disease that would surely land me in the city hospital, and once I would be outside the prison walls— in my fertile imagination—I saw myself free as a bird.

Thus, grimacing with pain and complaining of my ailment, I went to the Jewish doctor, who readily diagnosed that I was seriously ill, directing the policemen to have me examined by the German Medical Director. My instructions were to present myself at a certain place at half past nine in the morning from where the Jewish policemen would escort me to the Medical Director's office for an examination. Anxiously, I awaited the hoped-for hour, thinking that freedom was just around the corner. I showed up at exactly nine-thirty, but to my disappointment, I found no one there. I surmised that the Jewish policemen had left early intentionally, since they suspected me of wanting to escape and did not want to bear any of the responsibility.

I faced a dilemma. What was I to do? To go and see the doctor by myself was no simple matter. First, walking the camp grounds without a permit was strictly forbidden. Second, by the time I would find the doctor's office, which was quite far away, it would be past the twelve o'clock closing time of his office. Third, I was not on the sick list, thus the doctor surely would not want to see me. After mulling it over for a long time I decided to go to see the German doctor on my own. I had nothing to lose. Who knows? Maybe I'd be successful. In order to win, one had to take a chance.

I started walking, asking people for some directions, and

without being stopped even once, I arrived at the doctor's office well before the noon closing hour. After giving me a cursory examination, the doctor issued an admission card to the municipal hospital. I was elated; I considered myself the luckiest man alive.

I went back to work, and when a few days passed and nothing happened, I approached the Jewish police inspector Silberman, whom I knew from Vizhnitz.

"Since I have an official admission order, why wasn't I transferred to the hospital?" I asked him.

"The camp commandant has to countersign the admission order, and somehow he forgot to sign yours."

I recognized that something was amiss but kept quiet. For the next few days, Silberman tried to placate me, offering me various excuses, but I never saw the admission card again.

I had no choice but to go directly to the camp commandant. It was a dangerous undertaking, but I went anyway. At the entrance to the commandant's office, I was stopped by a German guard.

"What do you want?" he asked.

"I want to see the camp commandant."

He showed me in. The commandant, a tall, heavy-set man in an SS uniform, gave me a stern look.

"Why did you come to see me?" he asked.

I told him about the doctor's admission card. "Would you please let me have it so that I can go the hospital?"

"I signed that card a few days ago and gave it to Silberman," he told me.

Now I knew it was Silberman who was spoiling my chances for success. Nevertheless, I decided not to confront him with the facts, since it would serve no useful purpose. Clearly, he was a thoroughly evil person.

I spoke with another policeman I knew from Vizhnitz, a man named Yafek who was in charge of transporting the patients to the city hospital. I pleaded with him to try to do something for me to enable me to leave, and I promised him a decent reward for his efforts. Two days later, he came to me.

"You can go today," he said. "You'll use the name of a fellow who didn't show up for his scheduled doctor's examination."

I did not mind doing that, as long as it would get me outside the camp. I went to the location he indicated where I joined a group of sick people ready to go to the camp commandant's office to receive their admission cards to the hospital. Silberman was there to accompany us.

Throughout our march to the commandant's office, he did not say a word, but as we reached the building housing the office, he turned to me.

"Under no circumstances," he said, "will I let you go under an assumed name."

I begged him, I implored him to let me go in, but it was no use. Disillusioned and frustrated, I returned to work. My second escape attempt had turned sour.

CHAPTER 15

■

More Escape Attempts

LTHOUGH MY FIRST TWO PLANS ENDED IN FAILURE, I did not give up inventing new schemes for getting out of this hell. I couldn't just sit idly by and allow myself to be swept away by the Germans' diabolic designs; one must try to outwit one's enemies. It so happened that I found out that the prisoners in the adjacent barracks were going into town for the bath they should have had on their arrival. Here was my opportunity!

In the morning, when everybody streamed out of the barracks for roll-call, I hid in a corner in total disregard of the danger of getting caught, and *baruch Hashem*, no one came looking for me. Unobtrusively, I mingled with the prisoners of the other barracks who had not gone to work because of their scheduled trip into town. They were going to be taken there by truck at noon. I waited and waited. It was already well past twelve o'clock, with no truck in sight. The day went by, but the truck never showed up.

Again I had failed. But imagine my disappointment when in the evening the people of my barracks returned telling me that they were coming back from the Cracow ghetto . . . where they had been taken to have a bath! No doubt about it, this must have been Silberman's doing. Noticing that I had not shown up for work, he must have read my mind and switched the group going to the ghetto. Once again, he had gotten the better of me.

Still, I was not ready to concede defeat. I continued to concoct plans, waiting for the right opportunity, which was not long in coming. I learned that a certain group of Jewish workers was trucked from the ghetto into our camp each day and returned in the evening. Evidently, the Germans did this to save food and sleeping space.

"Since the guards at the gate know these workers," my informant added, "they don't check them at all."

That was all I needed to hear. If I would join this group, no one would notice me. Here was my ticket to freedom. "Silberman, this time I'm going to outsmart you!" I said to myself, half aloud. "This time you won't clip my wings."

It was the day before *Hoshannah Rabbah*.

That evening, I boarded the truck, blending in among the returning workers. My heart beat in joyous anticipation. Only thirty minutes more and my troubles would be over.

Sad to say, my joy was premature. Silberman must have gotten wind of my plan. When the truck reached the gate, instead of being waved through as usual, it was stopped. Looking outside, I saw a group of unfamiliar Germans. I found out later that they were the officers in the camp administration. My heart sank. Now I've had it, I thought.

Soon, I heard the familiar German command, "*Alle herunter!* Everyone, get out!"

Those with papers proving that they were living in the Cracow ghetto were lined up on the right, those without papers to the left. Apparently, there were others who had the same idea I had. The documented workers were released and continued on to the ghetto, while the rest were interrogated. Each man had a different excuse.

"My shoes needed repair."

"I wanted to take my clothes to the laundry."

And so forth.

While the Germans were busy questioning people, I sneaked away toward the camp. Unfortunately, one of the Germans noticed me in the distance and came chasing after me.

"Where do you think you're going?" he shouted furiously as he grabbed me.

"I forgot my identification card proving that I live in the ghetto," I answered defensively. "I just went to get it."

The German, seeing through my transparent lie, gave me a ringing slap in the face and dragged me back to the interrogation, where we were told to present ourselves at the office of the camp commandant the next morning at eight o'clock.

Needless to say, I did not sleep a wink that night. Promptly at eight, we were all assembled in front of the commandant's building where we had been taken under the supervision of Jewish guards led by Silberman. Silberman reported to the commandant that he was bringing in twelve attempted escapees. Two Polish guards in black uniforms emerged, guns strapped to their belts. One positioned himself in front of us, the other behind us. Then the commandant himself appeared.

With a quick wave of his thumb, he gave the command, "March!"

We followed the Polish guards, with the commandant trailing behind us on his bicycle. Panic-stricken, we whispered to each other, "They're going to shoot us. We've had it."

Conflicting thoughts raced through my mind. Is there still a chance of escaping? Forget it, I told myself. Just take one look at the armed guards surrounding you!

Our legs were shaking as we marched further and further away from the camp, the Angel of Death staring us in our faces. This is the end, I thought. No doubt about it.

Each of us reviewed his life, repented of his wrongdoings and prepared for the inevitable. We were still young. Some of us had wives and children. We had to accept Hashem's will with love.

At last, the command rang out, "Stop!"

The commandant ordered us to line up. He stepped out in front of us and thrust his hands in his pocket.

"You've tried to escape from this camp," he addressed us in cold, clipped words. "This is a serious crime. For this you deserve the death penalty."

I must admit I was scared. Soon, he'll squeeze the trigger, I thought, and the first victim will fall. Silently, I recited the words of the *Viduy* confession of sins. If only I wouldn't have to suffer much. I wondered when he was going to pull out his gun and start the execution. Then, thunderstruck and with wide-eyed surprise, we noticed that instead of a gun he pulled out a leather horsewhip. They weren't going to shoot us after all!

"Each of you will get twenty-five lashes!" the commandant continued.

He pulled the first man out of the line-up. The man began to stammer his lame excuses.

"Come on, bend over!" the German shouted.

With sadistic delight, he began flogging his defenseless victim. One . . . two . . . three . . . The poor fellow fell to the ground, writhing with pain. His heartrending screams stirred the commandant's thirst for blood, and he cracked his whip again, striking the man wildly on the head and face. When the commandant grew tired, the three Polish guards took over with visible relish.

Watching the spectacle, I was struck by the sheer inhumanity of it. But then I reasoned that it was a whole lot better than being shot to death. Still, it takes unusual toughness and fortitude to bear up under this kind of punishment. Figuring that the three goons would gradually grow tired, I slowly changed places, gradually moving further down the line until I ended up in the last position. But if Heaven has decreed something, there is no escape. Moving down the line, the brutal threesome did indeed become weary from administering the continuous beatings. But just as they were ready to slow down, out of nowhere there appeared a muscular, gorilla-like German hoodlum, strong as an ox, with a face reflecting sheer viciousness. Noting his comrades' fatigue, he volunteered to take over.

"Why don't you let me finish the job," he said, taking the horsewhip from their hands. "You fellows go and take a breather."

It just happened to be my turn to be whipped. Releasing all his pent-up sadism, he went to work on me, showing off his prowess to his exhausted buddies. I felt as though my skin was being peeled off; my body was on fire. He whipped me with such force that he could not complete the twenty-five lashes, giving up at seventeen, completely out of breath. Throughout the ordeal I suppressed my cries, not uttering a sound, which made him livid with rage.

"*Er schreit doch gar nicht!*" he angrily halled out. "He isn't screaming!"

When it was all over, they ordered us back to work. I don't know how I made it through the rest of the day. Still, I was happy to be alive.

In spite of the painful outcome of my last escape attempt, I lost neither courage nor faith in Hashem. I was determined to find a way to break loose, in one way or another.

Living conditions in the camp deteriorated from day to day, especially with regard to the food. My brother Yossel would send me food parcels, mainly bread, but often he could not find people who would bring in the parcels from the ghetto. In addition, the overcrowding and intermingling of different kinds of people fostered unsanitary conditions which resulted in a loathsome plague of lice. It was this scourge, more than anything else, that drove me to do my utmost to find a way out of this filth.

I devised the following plan. A short time before, a friend of mine had been released from the hospital, and he still had the admission card issued by the camp doctor. I decided to use this card for my escape. The prospects for success were not good, since even a card-holder was not permitted to move about freely in the camp without a guard watching him, but it was better than nothing at all. I reasoned that most of the German and Polish guards were unfamiliar with these regulations and the same held true for the guards at the entrance gate. I counted on being able to pass their inspection without too much difficulty. I took into account that staying in the camp held far greater risk.

The main problem, it seemed, was to get past the barbed wire enclosure, for there was one thing the camp guards knew very well—that no prisoner was to leave the camp grounds without a guard by his side.

I had a solution for this problem, too. In the labor camp, there was a special detail that worked outside the confines of the camp. Every day, the workers were driven to the work site accompanied by a Jewish guard named Kruger, whom I knew from Vizhnitz. I proposed to him that he take me along to work with his detail, reassuring him that even in the event I did not return, nothing would happen to him since all the men of his detail would be accounted for. I had in mind that once outside the camp I would catch the train to Cracow, since my bogus travel permit was still valid. I promised him a substantial reward for his cooperation, and he accepted the deal.

In the pre-dawn darkness, at wake-up time, I felt exhilarated. Today, I was going to be liberated! I joined Kruger's work detail, and went to the gate to be counted by the guards. One more minute and the gate would swing open. Suddenly, a Jewish guard named Gruenberg showed up.

"Hold it! Don't open the gate!" he told the gatekeeper. He shone his flashlight into everyone's face until he reached me. "Stop! Hold it right there! It's you I'm looking for."

I could not imagine how he had found out about my plan. I had kept it a deep secret, and except for my friend whose card I was using, no one had the slightest inkling of my plan. Could it be that Silberman, my arch-enemy, had been following me around? Had Kruger betrayed me?

Be that as it may, I was trapped once again. He'll probably

hand me over to the camp commandant who is surely going to shoot me dead, I thought, since he already spared my life once before. But even if he turned me over to the "black" Polish guards I would be beaten to within an inch of my life. Worst of all, I realized I was being pursued by bad luck; this was already my fifth failed escape attempt. Would I ever see an end to my troubles?

Now is not the time for self-pity, I admonished myself. I must *do* something. I made my move when Gruenberg, seeing that he had caught one fish, went to look for more would-be escapees. I slowly moved away from the work detail. But where should I go? Back to the barracks? Impossible! They'd find me within minutes. What should I do? I began to twitch like a chicken without a head.

Instinctively, I decided that I simply *had* to get out of this hell-hole, come what may. Either way I was a goner. I started running to the gate. The guards were busy checking all the work details rushing to work. Undetected, I sneaked to the barbed wire fence and scaled the wire, ripping my clothes and lacerating my legs. Blood ran down my legs, but I didn't even notice. As if possessed by a demon, I jumped down the other side. Down the road, I saw a group of workers marching in formation. It had to be Kruger's detail. I ran to catch up with them. They had only one more gate to pass through. When the workers noticed that a stranger had joined them they told Kruger about it. He came over to me.

"Sorry, I can't take you along," he said. "If I do, chances are that one of the workers will blow the whistle on me."

My voice shaking, I tried once more. "Come on, won't you let me come along anyhow?"

"Nothing doing!" he replied, lowering his eyes. "You've got to go back to the camp!"

I was cornered. Where could I turn? Back into the camp? A thousand times no. My mind was made up. I had to get out of this misery. I walked toward the outer barbed wire fence, the one that surrounded the entire camp, climbed it with my last ounce of strength, blood gushing from my wounds. I reached the top. I could smell the air of freedom, but I was not yet in the clear. Patrols of "black" guards circling the camp could shoot me on sight.

More thoughts raced through my head. If only I could get to a highway or any road at all. In front of me, I saw nothing but fields and pastures. My heart was pounding, my legs buckling. I was overcome with fright, as my lips repeated over and over, "*Ribono Shel Olam!* Please lead me on the right path and save me!"

Trudging laboriously through the freshly plowed fields, step by step, I finally came to a highway. But which way to turn, left or right? A mistake would land me right back in the camp again, for soon it would be daybreak and the guards would be able to spot me from a mile away. In the distance, I could make out a sprinkling of flickering lights. That must be Cracow.

Quickening my pace to get as far away as possible from the camp under the cover of night, I must have marched a mile or two, when suddenly I heard the clopping sound of horses pulling an approaching wagon. I went off the road, and peering into the carriage, I saw that the passenger was a well-dressed Polish gentleman.

"Sir, would you be good enough to give me a ride into the city?" I asked humbly.

"All right, hop in," the gentleman replied. He was truly an angel sent from Heaven.

On the way, we passed the main gate of the camp. I held

my breath, afraid that the guard might stop us to ask questions, but *baruch Hashem*, we passed without incident. Imagine, if this guard had suspected a Jew was passing him in this carriage, and an escaped Jew at that! For added insurance, since the sun was beginning to rise, I covered up my *Judenstern*, the yellow Jewish star on my jacket.

The Polish gentleman evidently had correctly assessed my situation.

"How come you're not afraid to travel around like this?" he asked me with unconcealed amazement.

I did not want to reveal my secret, fearing that he might report me to the police. I showed him my hospital admission card, and that ended the conversation.

After a thirty-minute ride, we arrived in downtown Cracow, where he suggested I get off since he was going in a different direction. I offered to pay him, but he graciously refused to accept payment. After thanking him from the bottom of my heart, I continued on my way.

The sun was already high in the sky, and I still had a long way to go. He had let me off on Lubitch Street, a distance of several miles from the ghetto. I was faced with a serious dilemma. Jews living in the ghetto were not permitted to be seen outside the ghetto except as members of a work detail under supervision of German or Polish guards, and here I was walking the Cracow streets all by myself, liable to be stopped and interrogated by any passing German or Pole which would mean certain death. I prayed to Hashem that He should help me to reach the ghetto safely.

Walking confidently so as not to arouse any suspicion, I reached the ghetto without encountering any obstacles. Now I faced my last hurdle before entering the ghetto—passing the checkpoint at the main gate. The guard there knew that without a special permit, no Jew was allowed to walk around alone outside the ghetto.

Approaching the main gate at Zgadi Square, I noticed two Polish guards, a sight that made my hair stand on edge. My life hung in the balance. I'll need Hashem's protection so that they won't ask me too many questions, I thought tremulously, for if they catch me, my next stop will be the Auschwitz death factory. With a self-assured gait, I started to walk toward the checkpoint, holding the crumpled note I had received from my friend, ready to show it. Seeing me step forward so confidently, they assumed I must have a special permit. When I reached the gate and waved the permit in their faces, they did not even bother to look at it but motioned me to go on in. To me, it was truly a miracle.

At long last, I found myself inside the ghetto walls. It was seven-thirty in the morning. The square was swarming with people assembled for work details. Among the workers, I recognized the detail that came to work in our camp every day. Approaching them, I told them about my escape and handed one of them the permit, asking him to return it to my friend.

They, in turn, related to me what had happened in camp after my disappearance. Gruenberg, who arrested me at the gate during my escape attempt, gleefully reported the news to his boss Silberman. But when they came looking for me, they found that I had disappeared. All guards were sent on a search, but they came back empty-handed. On the assumption that I surely must be hiding somewhere on the camp grounds, they turned over the entire camp in an attempt to catch me. Ironically, while they were searching, I was having breakfast in the ghetto.

Silberman and Gruenberg could not get over the

disappointment of having their prey get away; it was beneath their dignity to admit such blatant failure. Trying to save face, they spread the rumor that I had been arrested by the camp guards and that I was already in the custody of the German police. My friends were deeply depressed; they knew only too well the meaning of this. However, during the lunch break, their sadness turned to joy when they learned the truth from the workers I had met in the ghetto. Here was tangible proof of the lies and deceptions Silberman was trying to foist on them in an attempt to cool his anger and save his reputation.

From Zgadi Square I went straight to my brother Yossel's apartment. He was staying in the ghetto for the sole purpose of helping me while I was in the camp. I lack the words to describe our happiness when we met; after so many fruitless attempts, I had lived to be reunited with him. I sent a telegram to my mother in Bochnia, letting her know about my escape. Of course, I could not go there, since the Bochnia apartment was the first place the police would come looking for me.

Staying in the ghetto was also fraught with danger. I was likely to be arrested before long, since I had no residency permit. The Jewish police often conducted searches, since many escapees were hiding out with relatives. Besides, the camp guards occasionally visited the ghetto, and they might find me.

I had some pull with Shimon Spitz, the well-known official who worked for the Gestapo. Spitz had sent thousands of Jews to their deaths, but he had recently wanted to make amends. He arranged to have a Gestapo seal placed on my Bochnia residency paper which made it legal for me to stay in the Cracow ghetto.

The next several weeks, I stayed in Cracow, until one day I received a telegram from my mother urging me to come home. Concerned about her well-being, I left immediately. However, the telegram turned out to be merely a mother's ploy to bring her son home. Noting that lately no one had come to look for me, and since generally things were more quiet in Bochnia, she had sent the telegram to induce me to return there.

Back in the labor camp, Silberman continued his ruthless regime, but not for long. His best friends informed against him, reporting that he traded in foreign currencies, which happened to be true. On his frequent visits to Cracow, he engaged in this kind of business, amassing a great deal of money in the process. The camp commandant launched an investigation, and in a search of Silberman's living quarters, incriminating evidence was found. The Germans put him on trial and executed him. Soon thereafter, the camp itself was dissolved, and all inmates were sent to Auschwitz.

A short time after the Belzer Rebbe's escape from the Cracow ghetto, the Germans issued a decree ordering the entire ghetto population, young and old, without exception, to leave the ghetto. Included were also the members of the Jewish police and the Jewish Gestapo lackeys. Cracow was to become *Judenrein*, free of Jews. The Jews were to be housed in the wooden barracks that had been erected at the outskirts of the city. People were directed to present themselves at the main gate at the appointed time where they found Jewish, German and Polish policemen waiting for them. After being loaded on trucks, they were transported to the barracks of a camp, cynically called Jerusalemska. Adding insult to injury, the Germans erected the majority of the barracks on the grounds of the new Jewish cemetery after removing the gravestones.

On the day of the expulsion, the only thing the Jews were permitted to take with them was a knapsack with some food. The knapsacks were carefully examined to make sure no children were hidden in them. The camp was meant only for able-bodied people who could be put to work. Children had to be left back on the road, where they were gathered up by the Germans. The scene of parents forced to leave their small children behind was heartrending; they knew that their little ones were doomed to die. The wailing and shrieking of the fathers and mothers could make one's heart bleed, but not the hearts of the bloodthirsty German beasts. There were those who refused to be separated; they were killed along with their children. My sister-in-law, unable to part from her only child, placed herself among the children and was shot together with the children.

On this fateful day, the once proud Jewish community of Cracow came to an end. For many hundreds of years, it had been a vibrant center of Torah study, charity and acts of kindness. It vanished without leaving a trace. Twenty thousand Jews were transferred to this camp where their number dwindled from day to day at the hand of the *Lagerfuhrer*, Commandant Goett, a sadistic monster who was eventually tried as a war criminal and hanged. The remaining Jews in the camp were taken to the gas chambers in Auschwitz.

CHAPTER 16

■

Trouble upon Trouble

NOW THAT I WAS BACK IN BOCHNIA, I LIVED IN CONSTANT fear of being caught and sent back to the camp. The members of the Judenrat and the Jewish police were well aware that I had been carried off to a labor camp, and seeing me here in the ghetto would undoubtedly arouse their suspicion. But I learned to live with anxiety, and with the hope that everything would somehow turn out well in the end.

Just when things seemed to settle down somewhat, disaster struck again. A few days after my arrival in Bochnia, we heard from Binyamin Landau, a friend of the family, that someone had tipped off the Germans that Yossel was dealing in foreign currencies—which in fact was true. The informer was the notorious Shmuel Brodman, whose denunciations had caused the deaths of thousands of people. Brodman held an official position with the *Devisenstelle*, the Bureau of Trade in Foreign Exchange in Cracow, and as was so common among betrayers of his kind, he eventually met his violent end when he was shot by a German officer whom he had served faithfully for a number of years.

From our sources, we learned the exact time Herr Werner, the head of this Bureau, was due to arrive in Bochnia to arrest Yossel. It was to be on Friday. Anticipating his imminent arrival, we decided to eat our *Shabbos* meal during the day. We had hardly seated ourselves around the table when we saw Werner's car pass our house on its way to the Judenrat building. Any moment now, the Jewish police would come barging in. It was time for us to make a quick exit.

We left our table, and without losing a second, we were outside. They were actually coming only to get Yossel. From my own experience, however, I knew that if they didn't take Yossel they were likely to take me in his place, so I was forced to join him in flight. We reasoned that they would not take our mother, an elderly lady, and leave my two-year-old daughter unattended in the house.

We ran silently through the lengthening shadows, giving a wide berth to the Judenrat building which was close by. According to plan, we headed straight for the home of Abba Rosenzweig, a childhood friend of mine who lived nearby, where we would hide out until we found a way to escape from their clutches. Abba and his wife welcomed us graciously and offered us the room in the back of the house.

Meanwhile, the sun began to set, *Shabbos* drew near, and we prepared to *daven Minchah*. Just as we concluded the *tefillah*, Mrs. Rosenzweig entered and told us that she had just received a visit from Dr. Rosen, the chief of the Jewish police, accompanied by a Jewish policeman named Feder.

"Is Friedman in your house, by any chance?" Dr. Rosen had asked.

"I don't know what you're talking about," she had replied calmly, without blinking an eye. "He's not here."

They had evidently believed her, because they left without searching the house. Somehow, however, they had made the connection between us and Rosenzweig, and there was a real possibility that they might return. We decided to move down into the cellar, thinking that they would not search there.

In the cold and dark cellar, we sang *Kabbalas Shabbos*, after which we ate the savory meal our hostess brought down for us. Spending *Shabbos* as fugitives hiding underground added a bitter taste and dampened our spirits considerably. We stretched out on a few boards and tried to get some sleep, but suddenly, there was a scraping sound and Mrs. Rosenzweig came down the stairs.

"I'm afraid they'll come back, and if they find you we'll all be killed," she whispered in a trembling voice. "Please understand, I'm asking you to have mercy on us and leave. The Judenrat people know you are a good friend of ours, and they are sure to come and search our house."

We assured her that we understood completely, and then we slipped out of the cellar. For a while, we just sat in a darkened corner of the courtyard, not knowing where to turn. We climbed across the fence into the adjacent courtyard hoping to spot a hiding place there, but all we could find was an outhouse, which was liable to be used at any time—not a good hiding place. But as we drew closer, we noticed a small crawl space above the outhouse, and we squeezed into it. The cold was bone-chilling. To make matters worse, a sudden

135

downpour soaked us to the skin. What would become of us? We surely could not stay there after daybreak. We had no alternative but to ask to be allowed back into the dark cellar.

The night went by peacefully. In the morning, after we stretched our aching limbs, my friend Rosenzweig appeared and told us that all through the night the police, on orders from Werner, had searched the homes of all our friends and relatives. My mother and my brother Shimon had been taken hostage, notwithstanding that the little child was left alone in the house and Shimon was an amputee. How could they do a thing like this? We were dumfounded and completely unnerved by the news. How could Mother withstand all the torment? Also, the thought that they had made an all-out effort to catch us struck a deep fear in our hearts.

I got in touch with Moshe Schoenfeld, a man we could trust, and he kept us abreast of the situation. At the close of *Shabbos*, Schoenfeld told us that the hunt was still in progress while at the same time, the Germans were pressuring my mother and brother to reveal our hiding place. They, of course, had no idea of where we were hiding, since we had never discussed our plans with them.

We finally decided that Yossel would go to Cracow, which at the time had not yet been liquidated. After all, how long could he hope to stay hidden in the cellar? In Cracow, on the other hand, he could easily blend into the crowds and disappear. But getting out of Bochnia would not be easy. According to Schoenfeld, a special policeman had been posted at the station to arrest me in the event that I tried to leave Bochnia by train.

Somehow, I made it back to my house to remove all our hidden valuables, gold, diamonds and foreign currency. I took the entire treasure with me to the cellar where I divided it evenly with Yossel; so that if one of us would get caught, at least something would be saved.

In preparation for the trip, Yossel removed his yellow *Judenstern*, a "crime " punishable by death, and after a tearful good-bye, he went on his way.

A few days later, I received a letter in which he wrote that he had made it safely to Cracow. He did recognize the Jewish policeman Shlomo Greiber stationed on the platform, but since he mingled with the Poles—not wearing his Jew patch—Greiber paid no attention to him.

The Germans had good reason for selecting Greiber for this assignment. They knew that they could rely on him to do his job and not accept a bribe the way other policemen would. His cowering loyalty to the Germans bordered on insanity, to the extent that during the first extermination *Aktion* in Bochnia he personally led his sickly aged parents to the trucks to be transported to Botchkov where they were machine-gunned and hurled into a mass grave while still alive. He also placed his teen-aged son and daughter on the train to be taken to the Belzec death camp.

"It won't hurt them a bit to do a little work for the German Reich," the callous Greiber had said. "Nothing is going to happen to them." Greiber's actions convinced hundreds of Jews to voluntarily join the transports that were going to take them to "work."

I was happy to hear that Yossel was relatively safe. Now our entire family was scattered about—my mother and my brother Shimon in prison; my brother Yossel in Cracow; my infant daughter at home, being cared for by Shimon's wife; and I sitting here in the icy, dark cellar, living in constant fear, numb with cold. For the first time in my life, I was dependent on others to sustain me. It was a chastening experience to say the least. The Rosenzweigs tried to make my stay as comfortable as possible, seeing to it that I lacked nothing. Still, the situation was precarious. We prayed for Hashem to have mercy on us.

CHAPTER 17

■

The Second Raid

AFTER THE FIRST EXTERMINATION *AKTION*, ONLY A FEW hundred Jews remained in Bochnia. Over the following three months, however, their number gradually increased to five thousand, due to an influx of people from other ghettos that had been liquidated. Bochnia had a reputation of being a "favorable" place; compared to other cities, its SS men were more "humane." One could talk to them, and for a price, one could get them to do favors, and even when orders for an extermination *Aktion* came straight from Berlin, the killing did not reach an unbridled climax—if they had been paid off.

Rumors to the effect that another *Aktion* was in the offing created panic among the ghetto population, and the conflicting versions were the main topic of conversation. The wounds of the first *Aktion* were still fresh, and an atmosphere of foreboding pervaded the ghetto. I was not sure what to believe, but to be on the safe side, I decided to prepare a bunker for the Rosenzweigs and myself, for once the *Aktion* was blazing, it would be too late for that.

Building a bunker while being locked up in a dark cellar presented a problem. My solution was to build it underneath the cellar. The Rosenzweigs procured the necessary materials and tools, and I buckled down to work. During the daylight hours, I was busy excavating, while at night, the Rosenzweigs carried the dirt into the courtyard, spreading it around evenly so as not to arouse suspicion that a bunker was being constructed. Things like that were best kept secret.

Digging in the cramped cellar was not easy; nevertheless, after a few days of work the job was done. The bunker was fairly small, five and a half feet long, three feet wide and six feet deep. I left some earth along the wall to serve as a bench and installed a ladder for getting in and out. I covered the floor of the cellar with ashes from the furnace to make it look uniform. For the ceiling I used boards, leaving a man-size opening for an entrance. The boards were covered with earth and a thin layer of ashes on top to blend with the ashes on the floor of the cellar, making the bunker almost impossible to detect. A few more boards I scattered on the roof of the bunker to dampen the resonance created by walking on the hollow space of the bunker. For added safety, I built a large pile of lumber, tying a cord around it that could be pulled from inside the bunker, so that after we were in the bunker, we could yank the cord, causing the pile to come crashing down on the bunker entrance. A final test-run proved the effectiveness of the system. Although I was quite proud of my engineering feat, I gladly would have done without it.

Dark clouds were gathering; things were coming to a head. No doubt about it, the *Aktion* was imminent. My bunker gave me a semblance of security, but I could not relax knowing that my mother and Shimon were held captive in the Judenrat building and that, as a rule, prisoners were the first victims of any *Aktion*.

The ghetto was buzzing with rumors. The *Aktion* was only a few hours off. Throwing caution to the wind, I left the cellar and went to the Judenrat to try to have my mother and brother released. It was early in the morning, the streets were quiet, and except for Jewish policemen patrolling the ghetto, not a sound could be heard. I was frightened, but I kept my mind focused on saving my mother and brother.

In front of the Judenrat building, I saw workers and their dependents being loaded on a truck to be taken to safety until after the *Aktion*. They were escorted by Simchah Weiss of the Judenrat, under the watchful eyes of an SS sergeant.

I approached Weiss and tearfully implored him to have pity on my mother and brother.

"I give you my word," I promised him, "that after the *Aktion* is over they will come back voluntarily."

"Nothing doing," he answered callously, his words piercing my heart like a dagger.

As I was speaking to Weiss, Dr. Rosen, the chief of the Jewish police, suddenly emerged.

"Ah, there you are!" he pounced on me. "You're the one we've been looking for."

I trembled like a leaf. Now I'm doomed, I thought. Rosen was a vile character, but I had never believed he would stoop this low. There was no chance of escape, since the SS man standing next to him would surely grab me. Hoping against hope, I pleaded with him to let me go, not to send me to a certain death. My supplications must have touched his heart, for unbelievable as it may sound, he let go of me and turned away.

I recognized that any attempt at saving my mother was doomed to failure. I would simply wind up in the cell along with her. Returning to the bunker, I found my sister-in-law waiting anxiously, worrying that the worst had happened to me.

We now began preparing in all seriousness, and after moving provisions, candles and blankets into the bunker, we settled down for a stay of a few days until the storm would blow over. My baby daughter received a sedative since her crying might betray us. But the thought of Mother and Shimon in prison haunted me; would I ever see them again? I had done all that was humanly possible, not hesitating to risk my life. Now Heaven had to rescue them.

The bunker was shut tightly. At first, the candles provided some light, but after a few hours, the air became so stifling that they went out, leaving us in total darkness. We went into a fit each time we heard steps outside, thinking the Germans were coming to get us.

After thirty-six hours in the bunker, we began to hear people moving about in the street, talking to each other, a sure sign that the *Aktion* had run its course. I slipped out of our hiding place and went out into the street where I saw the workers returning to their homes. Without wasting a minute, I rushed over to the Judenrat building to find, much to my surprise, that Mother and Shimon were alive, although Mother's health was in a precarious state. She was not in her cell but lying in critical condition in an adjacent building.

Slowly, I learned the details of how they had survived the ordeal of the *Aktion*. It had been a terrible *Aktion*, although a much smaller one had been expected. People with connections to the SS had insisted that Bochnia would be spared, since it had been arranged with the SS that any *Aktion* that might be launched would be only a sham. Indeed, this may have been the reason Landau assured me on the night before the *Aktion* that no harm would come to anyone. But once the *Aktion* was under way things got out of hand. Hundreds of people were killed at random, and most of the ghetto population was carried off to the gas chambers in open freight cars. After the *Aktion* was over, the streets ran red with blood and were littered with bodies and human limbs, *yarmulkas, tzitzis* and personal effects. It was a ghastly sight. And this was supposed to be a "mild" *Aktion*, compared to the first one.

When Shimon heard of the impending *Aktion*, he did not sit still but built something like a bunker right there in the basement where they were locked up. He found a pile of heavy boards which he stacked up against a wall, leaving an empty space underneath. With his one good hand, he then proceeded to break all the door locks, making it appear as though they had broken out, so that the Germans would not look for them inside. The two of them survived by hiding beneath the boards for the two days of the *Aktion*. However, upon emerging from the bunker, Mother succumbed to the aftereffects of two days of sheer terror without food or drink and fell into a coma, hovering between life and death. Since there was no decent bed in the basement jail, the police agreed to have her transferred to a neighboring house.

My brother Pesachyah and his three children survived by hiding in the same bunker they had used during the first *Aktion*. We were elated that, unlike during the previous *Aktion*, this time our entire family had lived through the deadly raid. After recovering somewhat, Mother was returned to the prison.

However, our happiness was shortlived; in fact, it lasted no more than one day.

Since Shimon had broken all the locks he could not be kept in the Judenrat cellar for fear that he might escape. Instead, they kept him in an office under constant police guard. During the night, other people who had been taken into custody were brought into this office. Among them were two teenage boys who had been working for the Gestapo in Cracow. These boys burglarized the cabinet of the Judenrat office, carrying off all the treasures that were kept there, such as tea, coffee, sugar, cocoa and wine. In the morning, when Dr. Weiss, the Judenrat boss, discovered the burglary, he ordered an investigation. All the people being held in the office were severely beaten, but no one confessed to the crime. Shimon's defense of having been under constant police guard did not convince them. Weiss was furious. He sentenced the two boys from the Gestapo to be shot to death, insisting that it was only they who could have pulled off the burglary. Fuming with rage, he included Shimon with the burglars, condemning him to death as well.

I did not know what had transpired, but Binyamin Landau, our family friend, told me that Shimon had been sentenced to death. I refused to believe it; I could not imagine why he deserved to be shot. However, in the afternoon, when I brought their meals, the reality struck me with full force.

"Shimon has been taken away," Mother informed me. "I don't know where they've taken him or why he was moved."

I didn't tell Mother what I had heard, but my thoughts were in a turmoil. What could I do to save Shimon?

On my way home, I saw Dr. Rosen, escorted by two

policemen. The policemen approached me.

"We have orders from Dr. Rosen to arrest you," they said.

I had no choice but to come along. In the courtyard of the Judenrat building, I met Binyamin Landau.

"Could you find out why they're holding me?" I asked him. "And please try to get me out of this mess."

"Don't worry," he replied. "It doesn't mean a thing."

Before long I found myself in the same cellar with Mother.

"What are you doing here?" she asked.

"I wish I knew," I answered, sighing.

Shimon was not there any more, but I could hear him screaming with pain from the brutal thrashing he was getting at the hands of a Jewish guard from the Plashow camp who just happened to be in the ghetto. His shrieks were heartrending. The situation was desperate. Who was there to intervene for me, Mother or Shimon? Who was going to take care of my little daughter? What if they included me with the burglary suspects? I was caught in a trap; there was nothing I could do.

A short while later, Dr. Rosen entered and scrutinized the twenty or so prisoners. He stopped in front of me.

"Go on home," he said. "I don't want to have you on my conscience."

These words gave me an indication that I had been slated for execution along with the others. I said an aching good-bye to Mother and went home. Only then did I find out what had transpired.

After my arrest, Shimon's wife had hurried over to Binyamin Landau and told him about my capture. Knowing of the planned shootings, he gathered why I had been arrested. He rushed over to the Judenrat and explained to the officials that I was completely innocent of any wrongdoing. Since he was on good terms with them, his intercession worked, and Rosen let me go. Thus did Landau save my life. (Unfortunately, this compassionate and kindhearted person eventually perished in the concentration camps.)

As soon as I was free, I tried to find out about Shimon's fate. The news was bad. The guards at the ghetto told me, "About half an hour ago, they led Shimon through the gate and transferred him to the German police." I felt as though someone had hit me over the head. I knew this meant death.

It was already dark, but I still tried to do something, anything at all to save his life. But it was in vain; no one was willing to help me. It was almost midnight when I met Landau. I pleaded with him to have mercy on Shimon and his expectant wife. He promised to do all he could, and I stayed home hoping for good news. An hour later, Landau came back empty-handed. He had tried everything, but the Germans absolutely refused to release Shimon. My brother's fate was sealed.

The following morning—it was Friday, the 4th of Shevat, 1943—the Germans took Shimon to the cemetery where they murdered him. I simply could not bring myself to convey the appalling news to my mother and his wife, but they found out somehow. Mother was devastated but accepted his death as a divine decree and sat *shivah* in the Judenrat prison.

Gradually, Mother's health improved, but there was no chance of getting her released, no matter how hard I tried. The officials at the Judenrat argued that if Werner had personally ordered her arrest only he could order her release. Not until six weeks later was she released.

CHAPTER 18

■

Yossel Is Arrested

W HEN MOTHER CAME HOME FROM PRISON, I WAS jubilant. Our joy was all the greater since it seemed the police also had dropped the case against Yossel. But our joy was premature. Early one Friday morning before breakfast, we received a visit from Guter, the messenger of the Judenrat.

"You are to come along with me to the Judenrat," he ordered.

When I entered the office of Judenrat Chief Weiss, I found him relaxing on his couch over a breakfast consisting of fresh buttered rolls and a steaming cup of hot chocolate, a luxurious meal during the war years. And why shouldn't he? At the expense of the tormented Jews, he could allow himself to live like a king. With Weiss was a stocky German in civilian clothes who addressed me in a heavy Bavarian dialect.

"*Wie heisst du?*" he asked. "What's your name?"

I gave him my name.

"Where do you work?"

I went weak in the knees. Was this the camp commander of Rakowitz, the labor camp from which I had escaped? He certainly resembled him. I tried telling him that I was registered with the local labor detail. He asked Weiss to verify my answer, which, of course, he did not.

"*Warum hast du mich angelogen?*" he demanded. "Why did you lie to me?" Without waiting for an answer he slapped me good and hard to almost make me lose my balance. Then he asked, "Do you know somebody by the name of Tannenbaum?"

All of a sudden, everything became clear. Putting two and two together, I surmised that Yossel had probably been arrested, since Tannenbaum had business dealings with him.

"*Jawohl,*" I replied. "Yes, I do."

"Do you know where he lives?"

"*Nein,*" I replied. "No."

"How come?" the German wondered. "After all, he's a friend of yours, and he has visited your home many times."

"I've never had anything to do with him," I said.

Each question was accompanied by a dose of kicking, smacking and pounding. He was quite skilled at inflicting punishment, so much so that with his first beating he knocked out most of my teeth and sent me flying clear across the room. Witnessing the scene, aside from Weiss, were Rosen, who later was appointed head of the Judenrat, and his wife.

"If you don't tell the truth you'll be shot," they kept warning me as they stood alongside the German.

I stubbornly kept my mouth shut, knowing what would result from my disclosures; this was one thing I did not want to have on my conscience. Seeing that he was not making any headway with me, the German instructed Rosen to have Tannenbaum brought in at once. (Apparently, he had known Tannenbaum's whereabouts all along, and he had only wanted to determine the extent of my involvement with him.) Meanwhile, the police arrested my mother and several people from Melitz, Tannenbaum's home town, for the purpose of interrogating them. When they all stated unequivocally that they did not know where Tannenbaum lived, the German ordered them put behind bars. And so my mother was back in the same prison she had left just a short while before.

Turning to me, the German asked, "Do you know where your brother Joseph is?"

"No," I said.

"Do you keep up a correspondence with him?"

"No," was my firm reply.

He then pulled out a letter written in Hebrew from his briefcase and held it under my nose.

"Tell me, who wrote this letter?" he asked.

This time I could not deny it; my signature was there to prove it, black on white.

"Yes," I said. "I wrote this letter."

"Then why did you lie?"

He went at it again, punching and kicking without letup. By now, I recognized him as Werner, the head of the *Devisenstelle*, the Bureau of Trade in Foreign Exchange, a notorious brute who with his beatings could break down the strongest man to elicit secret information concerning currency transactions. Indeed, for some of his victims, the prospect of being shot didn't scare them half as much as the prospect of being beaten and forced to reveal information that would destroy friends and family, something worse than death.

As I stood there in the middle of this hellish scene, I was filled with despair. All the beatings I had endured were nothing compared to the distress I felt on learning that Yossel had been captured and a bitter fate awaited him.

Meanwhile, Rosen entered and reported that he was bringing in Tannenbaum and his wife. I was led to the jail in the basement where I found my mother.

"Woe is to us," she moaned. "Look what became of us. Yossel has been caught by the Germans. Who knows if he's still alive?"

I knew full well that Yossel was in deep trouble, since the informer had linked him to the most prominent currency dealers. Nevertheless, I encouraged Mother, telling her that Yossel would find a way to wriggle out of it.

A few hours later, a policeman read off the names of the people who had been released by Werner. Everyone went home, including Mother. Only I had to remain in jail. I was happy that at least my mother was free, and I felt confident that some day I, too, would be delivered from this misery.

I tidied up the basement to make it a little more liveable. Mother brought me delicious food for *Shabbos*, a blanket, a *Gemara* and *Shabbos* candles. In a way, I felt I was in Gan Eden. What more could I ask for? I even had a guest for *Shabbos*, a man who was arrested for stealing. I *davened Maariv*, ate my Friday night meal and bedded down on the hard board, falling into a deep sleep, exhausted as I was from Werner's beating.

No sooner had I fallen asleep than the squeaky sound of a key opening the door lock woke me up. A few more prisoners were brought in, but because of the dark I could not tell who they were. As the night wore on, we were joined by more and more prisoners. Among the voices in the dark, I recognized that of an acquaintance of mine, Lebovitz from Cracow.

"Hey, is that you, Lebovitz?" I asked.

"Yes."

"What brings you here?"

"Believe me, I have no idea."

Eight more prisoners were added to our cell, while several women were placed into the adjoining room. From time to time, one of the prisoners was taken out, to return after a while, his face beaten beyond recognition. Upstairs in the Judenrat, they were being interrogated in the presence of Simchah Shapiro, the Cracow district head of the Jewish police, a faithful lackey of the Germans, a man who sent thousands of Jews to their death.

As I found out later, the new prisoners were suspected of belonging to an underground partisan movement engaged in recruiting new members in the ghetto. The members were furnished Aryan papers, enabling them to escape during an *Aktion*. Shapiro, having been tipped off, arrested the members of the underground unit and interrogated them in an attempt to make them divulge the names of other members. As usual, the investigation was conducted by means of savage beatings which left the victims more dead than alive. The agonizing screams could be heard from a distance. After the interrogation, it took two policemen to drag the unfortunates back to the prison cell. Friends and relatives of the victims crowded around the small window of the basement prison, reassuring them that they were pulling strings to get them released. But the prisoners knew better, no one ever emerged alive from Shapiro's claws.

Sure enough, at eight o'clock in the morning, the voice from hell in the person of Simchah Shapiro called out.

"*Alle heraus!*" he shouted. "Everyone outside!"

This was the dreaded phrase used by the SS during the *Aktion*. Through the small window, we could see a bus waiting to take the prisoners away. Two policemen came in to lead them outside while I was trembling with fear lest they include me in the transport as well. They spared me and my first partner of the night, the suspected thief, locking the door as they left.

A few minutes later, the door opened again and a policeman summoned my cellmate to come along. He tried to resist, knowing where he was being taken, but it was useless; he had to go. Now I really got scared, realizing that they were not taking only political offenders. Only when seeing the bus depart could I breathe a little more easily. As I found out later, the prisoners were taken to Cracow where every last one of them was murdered.

And so I was all alone again. The days went by, and I saw no chance of extricating myself from the trap I was in. Mother ran from one wheeler-dealer to the other, since I was truly innocent of any wrongdoing. They put in a good word for me with Werner.

"As far as I'm concerned," Werner finally declared, "he is free to go."

And indeed, a few days later a Polish policeman entered my cell and told me, "You may go home now. You're a free man."

The joy that accompanied my release was dampened by our uncertainty about Yossel's fate. I made a concerted effort to learn his whereabouts, hoping to be able to intervene on his behalf.

After a great deal of effort, I learned that one afternoon, as Yossel was walking along the Cracow ghetto streets, a

Jewish policeman stopped him and instructed him to follow him to the police station. It seems that Brodman, the well-known informer, had betrayed him to the Germans. The Belzer Rebbe, who at that time was residing in the ghetto, was just then having a meeting with the two arch-villains Simchah Shapiro, chief of the Jewish police, and Shimon Spitz, an official in the political section of the Gestapo. The Rebbe used this meeting to intercede on Yossel's behalf.

"If you'll let him go free, I won't forget it," he told Spitz. "And I'll remember you forever."

But they turned the Rebbe down. "It's too late, nothing can be done any more," they replied harshly, implying that he was not alive any more.

This was a crude lie, for when the police led Yossel out of the ghetto to hand him over to the Germans, Shapiro personally escorted him to the gate to make sure Yossel would not slip away. During the investigation, they found that Yossel had Aryan papers, a crime far more serious than trading in foreign currencies. The beating he was subjected to went far beyond human endurance. The Bochnia and Cracow ghettos were buzzing with rumors that Yossel was no more. There were people who wanted to "cheer me up" with details of his tragic death. One version had him burned alive in a fiery furnace, another "eyewitness" reported seeing his bullet-riddled body being buried in the Cracow-Padgursz cemetery.

People deeply mourned his passing, since he was beloved by all circles for his charitable, kindhearted deeds and his honest and astute business dealings. And of course, he was an upright and pious *chassid*. I did my best to conceal these reports from Mother and to calm her and reassure her that Yossel would surely come home soon.

Personally, I did not lend much credence to the various stories, and I continued my search for his whereabouts. My efforts bore fruit, and I found out that he was being held in the most dreaded prison in Cracow, the Mantilupa fortress. Now I plunged head and shoulders into working for him, but it was useless. He was imprisoned in the political wing, which was headed by a German who could not be approached at any price. I was ready to spend a great deal of money, but nothing could be worked out.

Meanwhile, rumors about his death continued to circulate, but they were laid to rest when seven weeks later I received a letter from Yossel from Mantilupi Prison in which he asked for any kind of food and specifically for warm underwear and outer garments. The letter, which was in Yossel's handwriting, came as a complete surprise to me, for although I did not believe any of the rumors, a sense of doubt had begun to creep in that perhaps there was something to these tales after all. And now I had undeniable proof that "*od Yosef chai*," that Yossel was still alive. I quickly made a package of the desired articles and sent it with a trusted messenger to Cracow.

With documented evidence in hand that Yossel was still alive, I tried to convince all the people with the right connections to intercede for him. Unfortunately, it was futile, and except for this one letter, I never received another communication from him. After the war, I heard from a friend of Yossel's who was with him in Auschwitz that he had been assigned to an *Arbeitskommando*, a labor detail, and had worked in a coal mine, where he was killed in an unknown manner.

After Yossel's arrest, Mother was overcome with profound grief, becoming a pale shadow of her former self.

"Yossel is gone . . . Shimon is gone . . ." she would moan plaintively. This was her third child whose life had been taken by the Germans. Nevertheless, she consoled herself with the hope that she would see him again some day.

CHAPTER 19

The Ghetto of the Living

J UST WHEN IT SEEMED THAT THINGS COULD NOT GET worse, the situation deteriorated even more with the appointment of Captain Muller as the new camp commandant. Wanting to be innovative, Muller decreed that all Jews, men and women alike, would have to work. Those unable to work—the aged, infirm and children—would be separated. Workers were to live in Ghetto One, non-workers in Ghetto Two.

Without delay, a fence was erected dividing the ghetto into two sections, and guards were stationed all along the fence to prevent anyone from crossing over. One did not need to be told the meaning of Ghetto Two. Everyone knew that Germans didn't waste food on unproductive people; such people were expendable.

The new decree threw the small ghetto population into a panic. Everyone went looking for work. The general anxiety provided the Judenrat people with a wonderful opportunity to fill their coffers, and the price they charged for a job rose from day to day. Long lines would begin to form early in the morning in front of the Judenrat building. People would wait for hours on end to get any kind of job. But it was well worth it, for it meant residing in the "Ghetto of the Living."

Aside from the all-pervasive fear, the new decree created a great deal of confusion, since many people living in Ghetto One were forced to move to Ghetto Two and vice versa. On the other hand, if one family member was employed, the entire family was permitted to live in Ghetto One.

Our apartment happened to be located in Ghetto One, but since no one in the family held a job, we knew we would have to move to Ghetto Two. Needless to say, I abhorred the prospect of living there because of the ultimate fate in store for its inhabitants. Deep in my heart, I was convinced that the Germans would annihilate both ghettos, but not wanting to swim against the current, I applied for a job in order to retain the right to remain in Ghetto One. I hoped that my mother and my daughter would also be allowed to stay on my account. Ironically, I, who had always avoided any form of heavy labor, was now forced to seek it. And it was not easy to find a job. People with better connections had taken all the local jobs, and by the time my turn came, only one kind of job was left.

In the village of Domienitz near Bochnia, one hundred men were needed for a *Kommando*, a labor detail, to cut down timber. I was not too anxious to do this kind of heavy labor outdoors all day in the freezing cold. But if one has no choice one takes anything one can get—and even for this job I had to pay a pretty penny. On the basis of my working papers, I received a residency permit for Ghetto One for myself, my mother and my daughter.

On the first day of work, we gathered at the station and received a monthly railroad ticket. We waited and waited, but there was no train. We assumed it was because there was heavy snow covering the tracks. Seeing that no train was coming, the foreman announced, "Since our work site is only about five and a half miles away from here, I suggest that anyone wanting to do so should go on foot."

Part of the group refused to walk and went home. Although diligence is not one of my outstanding qualities, I reasoned that on the first day I'd better not show myself as being lazy. We began to march. It was cold enough to make your teeth chatter, but pacing along we warmed up a bit. (This march would prove to be extremely helpful a year later when I saved my life using this route.)

Plodding through fields and forests, we arrived at our site. The foreman stepped up onto a stump and began to make a speech. "The work you are going to do in this forest is for the SS. Therefore, you must work with dedication and appear on time every morning. Be sure never to be late or miss a day's work."

A fine speech, I thought, but I don't care. I'll do what's best for me.

We were divided into teams and assigned specific tasks. Each team was made up of five men—two men to saw the tree, one man with an ax to make sure the tree fell in the right direction, one man to peel off the bark and the fifth man to measure the felled tree and mark the dimensions on it. The foreman handed out the implements, and everyone chose the tool he liked best. Since I did not like any of them, I was in no hurry and waited until everyone had selected his tool. By then, there was no tool left for me. I joined a team of five men, and since I was carrying no tool, my presence was useless; I was "the sixth wheel," but I didn't care.

We were lined up and marched through the dense snow-covered forest. Our march took quite a long time, the biting cold freezing our hands and feet. Suddenly, we heard the sputtering sound of a motorcycle coming up behind us. Two German policemen! We were seized with deadly terror. Now it dawned on us, "That's why they brought us deep into this forest! They are going to finish us off."

The policemen ordered us to stop. They got off the motorcycle. We recognized one of them. It was Bogusch, the German who carried out all the executions in Bochnia and had boasted, "I get my biggest kick out of killing Jews."

Seeing this monster, we lost all hope. Everyone prepared for the worst, standing there in deathly silence. What was going to happen to us? Bogusch pulled out a sheet of paper from his briefcase and called out the name of one of the Jews.

"Is he here?" he barked.

"Yes," the foreman replied, ordering the man to step forward.

The two policemen grabbed him, placed him on their motorcycle and rode off.

Although our worst fears had not materialized, the entire incident left us in a state of shock. On our return trip, some Polish lumberjacks, who also worked in this forest, told us that in the morning two German policemen had brought a Jew along with them. They told the Jew to dig a hole, and when he was done, they told him to undress. Then they shot him and threw his body into the hole. It seems that the Jew had given all his belongings for safekeeping to a Polish acquaintance of his. But when he needed some money and asked the Pole to give it to him, the Pole had denounced him to the Germans. The lumberjacks gave us the murdered man's clothes and showed us where he was buried. Horrified, some of us broke down in tears. Someone said *Kaddish*, and then we went home.

This was my first day on the lumber *Kommando*. The following day, I did not go to work; I had had my fill from the first day. But ultimately, I had no alternative but to go back to the job, especially since the work was supervised by the SS.

The work was very tough. First, we were outdoors all day long, without even a drop of warm water to thaw our frozen limbs, and even worse, while sawing we had to get down right into the deep snow. Second, there was the ever-present danger of falling trees; it happened more than once that workers were injured by falling timber and narrowly escaped losing their lives. But worst of all was the SS guard, a barbarian with a frightfully vicious facial expression, who always circulated among the laborers, supervising their work. In the beginning, he would show people how to swing an ax or hold a planing tool, since obviously he was an expert forester. Every day, he would check to make sure that each team had cut its quota, and if he found anything not to his liking, he would vent his wrath on the workers; indeed, he was even better at giving beatings than at felling trees.

My team, too, was privileged to get a taste of his handi-work. One day, he suddenly came up behind us.

"Well, how much did you produce today?" he snarled.

Understandably, we did not have much to show, since no one could possibly meet his outrageous quota. One of us pointed to the trees we had managed to cut. Being an experienced woodsman, he realized at once that some of the trees had been cut the day before.

"Is that all you men cut today?" he asked sarcastically.

Trouble was brewing; his face was contorted with anger. But I, more than anyone else, had reason to be terrified; the others at least were holding their saws and axes, but I was standing empty-handed. Quickly, he picked up a heavy branch and told all of us to bend over a fallen tree trunk. He then beat us and beat us with all his might, breaking the heavy branch on our backs until we could no longer move.

Wonder of wonders, I got off with just a few minor slaps. The German, not satisfied with the thrashing he had given us, took out his revolver, loaded it—then put it back into the holster. Evidently, he wanted only to scare us.

Incidents such as these were daily occurrences. However, since the work was what kept us alive—or so most people thought—we had no alternative. Ghetto Two was considered the home of the living dead, whose occupants had a few more days to live at the most.

Although I never did a stitch of work, and only on rare occasions did I pick up a tool to get some exercise and warm up, I could not bear the aimless life of constant fear, especially since the SS man, at his whim, could finish us off without batting an eyelash. I came to the conclusion that, come what may, I had to get away from this cursed place.

I began by not showing up for work half of the time, not giving any thought to the German overseer's warning to shoot anyone absent from work. I never showed up on *Shabbos* or on Fridays since we would return after sunset. Nothing at all happened to me, and I thoroughly enjoyed each day I stayed away from work.

CHAPTER 20

■

Tightening the Screws

ONE FRIDAY, WHILE WALKING THE GHETTO STREETS, I bumped into Dr. Rosen, the Chief of Police, who called me over to him.

"How come you're not at work today?" he angrily asked.

Before I could answer him, he grabbed me and threw me in jail, but not without first giving me a sound lashing with his whipping cane. His furious thrashing reached a point where a policeman, unable to watch it any longer, simply took away the cane from him. Rosen then confiscated my working papers—documents without which one could not exist.

"I'm going to have you shot," he said matter-of-factly. "I'll make an example of you, so people will know once and for all what will happen if they don't show up for work."

No doubt about it, he meant what he said.

I was put in jail, expecting to spend *Shabbos* there, but as soon as my mother found out, she moved heaven and earth to have me set free. She had not yet recovered from her own ordeal, and now this!

In the end, thanks to the intervention of the Belzer Rebbe, I was released. The Rebbe, who at that time was staying in the Bochnia ghetto, sent a personal emissary to Rosen demanding that I be set free, whereupon he let me go that very same Friday.

Muller, the new *Lagerfuhrer*, organized the labor force into three divisions—*Wehrmacht*, workers for the armed forces; *Rustung*, workers for the weapon's industry; and *Zwangsarbeit*, forced labor. Every worker was provided with a white patch marked with the insignia of his division—W, R or Z—and stamped with the Gestapo seal. The patch, which measured two and a half inches by two and a half inches, had to be attached on your left side, so that you were labeled twice, a yellow Jew-patch on your right and the new patch on your left.

The new white patch was a "badge of life." Wearing it identified you as a worker, giving you a chance of survival; at round-up time, this patch would protect you. Of course, you had to pay a price for the white patch. The W insignia, meaning that you worked for the *Wehrmacht*, was the most sought after. Next was the R patch, and least desirable was the Z patch for *Zwangsarbeit*, forced labor. My forestry detail was assigned a W patch, because our work in the Domienitz forest benefited the *Wehrmacht*.

Now I had to find a way to get out of the harsh forestry detail. I tried pulling strings, spending a great deal of money, but it got me nowhere. It was out of the question; the Germans in charge of the Domienitz detail did not release any of their laborers. I was stuck, forced to go to work week after week. On our way to work, we suffered a great deal from the Poles who would often try to throw us off the speeding trains. But worst of all was working all day long in the freezing cold. It was simply unbearable. We sometimes managed to build a small fire, but it did very little to relieve the numbing, bone-chilling frost.

One icy day, we were huddled around the flickering fire, gazing into the darting flames and sadly contemplating the bleak prospects for our lives which were hanging by a thread. Then Bleicher, one of our buddies, softly began to sing the familiar tune of *Dos Stettele Brennt* (*Our Town Is on Fire*). His sweet, lilting voice touched our hearts, bringing home the gloomy reality of the lyrics. There was not a dry eye in the group.

Quite unexpectedly, we were told one day that the work in the forest was completed. That evening, before we returned home, the German supervisor called us together.

"The job is done," he curtly announced. "Don't come back tomorrow."

The work was finished, but it ended in tragedy. On our way to the train, a group of German soldiers coming from the other direction began to shoot at us. One bullet struck our Jewish foreman, critically wounding him. Our work in the forest, which had begun with bloodshed, ended in bloodshed.

Nonetheless, we were happy to be free from this backbreaking job. The drawback was that being without work we now had to move into the dreaded Ghetto Two. However, the Judenrat promised us new jobs inside the ghetto, since we had lost our jobs through no fault of our own. In the meantime, we could remain in Ghetto One. But when the *Lagerfuhrer* opened a new industrial plant, the Judenrat's promises proved to be just so much hot air. In order to qualify for one of the one thousand job openings at the new plant you had to meet one of the following criteria: you had to be a skilled craftsman, you needed "pull" or you were required to pay either cash or furnish machinery for the plant. I did not qualify on any of these counts, and in spite of the Judenrat's solemn promises, they gave the jobs to other people. I remained unemployed.

With the opening of the plant, the *Lagerfuhrer* issued a series of new decrees for Ghetto One, which was considered a "workers' camp." Husbands and wives were not permitted to live in the same apartment. They were permitted to see each other after work, for two hours only. Also, no private cooking facilities could be used. All workers were required to use the communal dining room.

The Jewish police, who were charged with the strict enforcement of these directives, patrolled the ghetto streets, keeping an eye on the chimneys to look for telltale smoke. If you were caught you had to pay a fine or were put in jail. If, on one of his frequent ghetto tours, the *Lagerfuhrer* himself would catch someone, he would personally give them a brutal beating. Sometimes, he would suddenly appear in the evening to make sure that no couple stayed together past the time limit. Couples caught violating the curfew were given a special dose of his unbridled fury, men and women alike.

With the issuance of the new ordinances, the separation between the two ghettos was intensified. Anyone caught in the wrong ghetto was arrested. All the "unemployed" living in Ghetto One were required to move to Ghetto Two along with their families, an upheaval that drove the ghetto population into a frenzy. Mother and my little daughter, together with my brother Pesachyah and his three children, were transferred to Ghetto Two. Luckily, they were assigned an apartment for themselves, whereas other families were forced to share the cramped living space of a tight apartment.

My situation was up in the air. I did not want to move into Ghetto Two because of the rumors regarding its probable destiny. Then again, staying in Ghetto One required a job, something I did not have. I decided to make my home in the woodshed in the courtyard of my building where I installed a bed and a small cabinet to hold my clothes and my possessions. I even had a "roommate," my friend Reuven Walkin from Oshpitzin who was in a situation similar to mine and whose company I enjoyed greatly.

During the day, we kept the shed locked up and just roamed around the ghetto. I dressed in my blue overalls, displaying the white worker's patch I still had from my Domienitz forest days, so that no policeman would ever dream of asking me for my worker's permit.

Now and then, I managed to sneak into Ghetto Two where I had to remove my white worker's patch. After barely subsisting on a starvation diet of bread and water in Ghetto One, I was elated to have a taste of Mother's cooking.

Slipping from one ghetto into the other was extremely risky, since the Jewish police rigorously guarded the fence. Guards watching the fence from observation posts outside the ghetto, waiting for their prey, shot anyone trying to sneak across, while other guards constantly patrolled the fence looking for breaks. All this was done on orders of the groveling Chief of Police Rosen who slavishly served the Germans beyond the call of duty.

On weekdays, I did not take any chances, but I did not want to miss spending *Shabbos* with Mother. The loneliness of the weekdays depressed me, aside from the constant fear of being discovered in my hiding place. Whenever I heard of an impending inspection, I asked my neighbors to place a padlock on the outside of the shed to mislead the Germans. Several times, they chased me, but I managed to elude them.

On *Purim*, as I was on my way to *daven*, a policeman stopped me, demanding to see my worker's permit. I had nothing to show him.

"You'd better come along with me to the Judenrat," he ordered.

I was in no mood to see Rosen, certainly not on a happy day like *Purim*. I made up my mind that I was definitely not going to sit in jail that day. As we were walking, I suddenly made a break for it and ran. He tried to catch me, but I was faster, dashing into one of the courtyards where I disappeared into a hidden corner. He soon gave up the chase. Now, that was a real *simchas Purim*, a real rejoicing of *Purim*!

Such incidents were daily events; my life in the ghetto was a series of terrifying experiences, not to mention the freezing cold in the drafty shed.

One *Shabbos*, when I was in Ghetto Two as usual, I woke up early to witness a terrifying scene. The ghetto streets were teeming with Jewish policemen, the outside fence was guarded by Ukrainians, and the German police was coming up in the distance. People were running in all directions, frightened out of their wits. Shouts of confusion filled the air.

"What's going on?"

"What are they going to do to us?"

Some tried to sneak out of the ghetto, across the outer fence, but they were brought down by deadly rifle fire. Inside Ghetto Two, all was quiet, the policemen walking about with icy calm. It was the stillness before the storm.

Mother went into the street and inquired of a policeman

about the aim of this *Aktion*. Although according to regulations he was not permitted to reveal any "secrets," he spoke to her nonetheless.

"Go home and don't worry," he told her. "Nothing is going to happen to you. They're not looking for your kind of people."

When Mother told me what he had said, I reasoned that "*miklal lav atah shome'a hen*—from the negative you can infer the positive." If they were not looking for her kind of people, it could only mean that they were looking for able-bodied men.

I realized that some of my friends living at the other end of the ghetto surely were not aware of what was in store for them. Quick as lightning, I ran to them and found them all sound asleep. I knocked on their window.

"Wake up, everybody!" I yelled. "Wake up! Quick! The house is on fire! There's an *Aktion* going on. They're grabbing young people!"

Jumping out of bed, they quickly got dressed. They had prepared a bunker and told me to join them. The bunker was quite primitive; a dummy wall with an opening for a man to pass through set apart the space for the bunker. After the men entered the bunker, the women blocked the opening with a heavy bookcase, making it impossible to detect. Inside, it was very tight. There was barely enough room to stand, and we had to hold back any movement, cough or sneeze, since the slightest whisper could be heard through the thin wall. We even had to hold our breaths.

There were five of us in the bunker, waiting with bated breath for what the day would bring. Hardly ten minutes passed when we could hear the fearsome voices of the Germans.

"*Sind Manner hier?*" they shouted. "Are there any men in here?"

"No," was the frightened reply.

That was not good enough for them. They proceeded to turn the entire house upside down, searching all the rooms. We almost died with fright; what if they moved the bookcase? After all, the system of building dummy walls was well-known. But Hashem was on our side, and they left without doing any harm.

However, the episode did not end here. Half an hour later, another group of Germans came in, looking for men. And so it continued, a long parade of visitors barging in at regular intervals, Jewish policemen and Germans, while the women kept us abreast of the goings-on.

A short while later, two trucks pulled up from the extermination camp Jerusalemska to haul off one hundred Jewish workers to the camp, which stood under the command of the notorious SS Obersturmfuhrer Goett. This camp, situated on the site of the Jewish cemetery of Cracow-Padgursz, held about twenty thousand Jews whose numbers dwindled from day to day in the wake of terrible bloodbaths. Goett was accustomed to ride through the camp every day on his white horse, shooting at random any Jew who crossed his path. These workers had to be replaced by fresh merchandise. At the present time, he needed one hundred laborers, and Ghetto Two was going to be the source.

Meanwhile, the quota was almost filled, but they simply could not round up the few workers they still needed to complete the quota for that day. Coming back with fewer than one hundred was out of the question. The hours passed. It was almost dark, and the quota still was not filled. The Germans found a simple solution to their problem. "Let's grab some men from Ghetto One."

It was easy. The men of Ghetto One did not dream of hiding out. After all, they were working for the *Deutsche Reich*.

Such was the fate of all the Jews, always living under the illusion that working for the Germans would afford them protection. But how was a Jew to fathom the bottomless depravity of the German nation?

At last, after long hours of painful waiting, we were told that the Germans had pulled out. Only then did we dare leave the bunker, but we were still afraid to go out into the street. At once, I sent a message to Mother who had been worrying about me all day, telling her of my whereabouts. We said our *Shabbos* prayers, thanking Hashem for saving us from this dreadful *Aktion*. Before we ended our prayers, Mother arrived in order to convince herself that I was indeed still here.

Life in the ghetto became more grim by the day. No sooner did you adjust to one decree than a new one was issued. According to the latest directive, all rooms, basements and attics in Ghetto One were to be completely emptied out. The Jewish police, which was in charge of implementing the program, dragged furniture and other possessions into the street, destroying it all in a huge bonfire. I still managed to transfer my things from the shed to Ghetto Two, and now I had no choice but to move there myself.

The *Lagerfuhrer* also ordered that a number of homes in Ghetto Two be set aside as children's homes, ostensibly to provide care for the children while the parents were at work. But the true reason was obvious; we were all too familiar with the German conception of "compassion" for Jewish children.

Everyone had an uneasy sense of foreboding; the daily directives foreshadowed deep trouble. Hardly a day went by without an inspection by high-ranking SS officers from the

Aussiedlungsamt (deportation department) to survey the scene.

In spite of these ominous portents, life in Ghetto Two continued calm and undisturbed. People got up at a comfortable hour, walked to *shul* at a leisurely pace, went for a stroll, attended a Talmud lecture in the afternoon and went peacefully to sleep as if nothing had happened.

In Ghetto One, on the other hand, life was hectic. You had to get up early and rush to work, but before that you had to be present at roll-call on Kowalska Street. From there you marched to your work site in German-style military formations, five abreast, under Jewish police escort. The work itself was harsh and oppressive, it broke you down both physically and mentally. When you came home at night you were too worn out to think about the future.

Most people were convinced that the work would keep them alive. After all, their labor was essential for the German war effort! Some people worked at manufacturing bomb casings and producing uniforms for parachutists. Others recycled clothing of the murdered Jews of the ghettos into garments for German men, women and children. They thought the German victory depended on their work. By planting such myths into their minds, the Germans turned the Jews into docile slaves who would not even think of ways to save themselves.

Much as I doubted that the occupants of Ghetto One would come out alive, to my mind the eventual deadly end of Ghetto Two was a foregone conclusion. I told Mother that in my view the ghetto would be terminated that summer, and I advised her to turn all our belongings into cash.

"Money might help get you out of a tight spot," I said, "but any object of value we'll have to abandon to the Germans."

Accordingly, we gradually began to sell to the Poles

171

everything we owned, our clothes, linen, tablecloths and so on. The actual sale was handled by brokers, since anyone approaching the Polish buyers was likely to be shot by the German guards. However, there were brokers who were willing to risk their lives for a profit of a few pennies. In this manner, I managed to dispose of all our belongings.

Regrettably, my prediction came true. In early *Elul*, both sections of the ghetto were liquidated, and there remained not one Jew in the once flourishing community of Bochnia.

Bochnia lived through three *Aktionen*, extermination raids, and after the third one, the city was *Judenrein*, empty of Jews. In all the killing raids, the Germans were assisted by the Jewish police acting on orders of the Judenrat, whose members reaped handsome profits from those about to die. For reasons known only to them, the Germans did not carry out simultaneous *Aktionen* in a number of towns. Perhaps they had only a limited number of the so-called *Einsatzgruppen*, the teams of professional killers. In any event, as a result of this policy, many Jews were able to evade the *Aktion* by finding refuge in another ghetto that was still occupied by Jews, in the hope of staying there until they would flee to another safe haven or—who knows?—the war might end.

The Judenrat people, well aware of these runaway stragglers, directed the Jewish police to watch the railroad stations for escapees from annihilated ghettos. Anyone who was caught was jailed in the Judenrat basement, under the pretext that they would have to stay there until they received a residency permit and found an apartment. Meanwhile, the Judenrat made inquiries regarding the financial status of the escapee and used the information to squeeze every last penny out of him. Not until their ravenous appetite for money was stilled did the hapless refugees see the light of day. This was one of the main sources of their wealth, since between one *Aktion* and the next, thousands of new refugees would arrive.

Another source of income for them was the sale of jobs in the Judenrat office or on the Jewish police force. Being listed on the staff of the Judenrat or the police was considered the best insurance against any harm during an *Aktion*. The cost of these positions ran into the hundreds of dollars. In reality, everything turned out to be nothing but wishful thinking. When the *Aktion* came, the Judenrat people as well as the police were annihilated along with all the other Jews. But until that fateful day they lived a life of ease and comfort on the backs of the oppressed and tortured Jews.

The Judenrat also earned large sums by demanding money from applicants for jobs in German factories. From time to time, the Germans would establish a new factory and would order the Judenrat to furnish laborers. Whenever this became known, a long line of job seekers formed outside the Judenrat office, who thought that a job would offer them protection. The Judenrat seized the opportunity to charge as much as twelve hundred *zlotys* for a worker's permit.

As we have seen, the Germans had a fiendish policy of extorting money from the ghetto population. Before an impending *Aktion* they would suggest that the Jews pay ransom in return for which the killing raid would be deferred. The Germans, intending to extract every last cent before sending the Jews to the gas chambers, placed the Judenrat in charge of the collection of the huge ransom. The Germans could rely on them to carry out their orders to perfection. The Judenrat did not disappoint the Germans.

CHAPTER 21

∎

The Final Raid

A S TIME WENT BY, MORE AND MORE JEWS BEGAN TO LOOK
for ways to get out of the ghetto. The latest trend was
to attempt to obtain foreign citizenship papers, or
even forgeries of foreign papers. A number of ghetto residents had received such documents from relatives abroad,
and when they showed their newly-acquired papers to the
Gestapo commandant in Bochnia, they were amazed at how
quickly and easily he granted the documents official recognition by signing them and attaching the Gestapo seal to them.
The bearers of such documents were given the status of
foreign nationals and, as such, were exempt from any anti-
Jewish laws and free to move about the country without a
special permit. They were allowed to live outside the ghetto
walls, and they were not required to wear the yellow *Judenstern*.

It goes without saying that such papers were extremely helpful, especially during an *Aktion*, since they were the ticket to get out of the ghetto.

The acceptance of the foreign affidavits spurred a flourishing business in such papers, which were sold at exorbitantly high prices. The main problem was establishing contact with someone residing in a foreign country. The mail was very slow and irregular; besides, all mail to and from foreign countries had to pass the censor, which made corresponding about passports and the like extremely hazardous.

Around this time, a Jewish organization was established in Prokatzim, near Cracow, which furnished such foreign documents and helped Jews escape to Czechoslovakia and from there to Hungary, where life was more secure. It was by no means a non-profit organization; in fact, they charged a very steep fee for their services. A number of non-Jews were involved in the work; they were needed for smuggling people across the border. Since many people could not legally travel to Prokatzim, they invented a method of transporting people to a point close to the border, from where they were smuggled to the other side.

A truck with a double floor was used, something akin to a moving bunker. Fifteen to twenty Jews were squeezed, like sardines in a can, into the space between the two floors. The truck then drove to a point near the Slovakian border where Poles were waiting to take them across. This escape route was used for quite a long time, saving the lives of hundreds of Jews from the Bochnia ghetto.

But nothing lasts forever. The escape route was shut down, thanks to informers. Several trucks were captured and their entire human cargo was shot on the spot. There were some daring drivers who ignored the command to stop and instead stepped on the gas, racing across the border at breakneck speed. As a result, the Germans barricaded with barbed wire all the roads leading to the border. After a number of people met violent deaths, the entire project was abandoned, and the search was on for new escape routes.

A Jew never sits still; he is always confident that if he searches hard enough he will find what he seeks. Since the foreign papers were recognized by the Gestapo, a dynamic enterprise was started producing spurious documents that looked more genuine than the real thing. An initial test was made, and when Gestapo chief Schoenberg validated the papers, production went into high gear. In order to avoid raising suspicion, people did not present the papers to Schoenberg themselves, using paid Jewish intermediaries instead. These intermediaries rapidly gained the chief's confidence, and before long, they were able to persuade him to do just about anything they wanted. Without asking questions, he would affix the Gestapo seal to any document they submitted, transforming the bearer into a legitimate foreign national.

Most of the documents received Schoenberg's endorsement through the efforts of his personal chauffeur, a Jew named Ferdinand. In this manner, many of the ghetto inmates were able to leave, and some of those who made it across the border wrote letters relating that they had settled in Hungary where life was unruffled and serene, just like in the good old days. Hearing all this, and knowing that the days of the ghetto were numbered, I felt the urge to try my luck in this direction. However, by the time I made up my mind, it was too late. The Gestapo chief was being inundated with a virtual torrent of documents, so that he refused to issue any further validations.

Terribly disappointed, I had no alternative but to leave the ghetto illegally. I had to get out, come what may. I had nothing to lose. I planned to escape by taking the train to Prokatzim and with the help of the Jewish underground to proceed to the Slovakian border. Having made up my mind, I proposed to my mother that she come along with me, together with my daughter. Taken by surprise by the unexpected proposition, she wrung her hands.

"What shall I do?" she moaned. "How can I take a chance like this? If I travel to Prokatzim without a *Judenstern*, my Jewish face will give me away."

With all the eloquence at my command, I tried to explain to her that we simply had no choice. An *Aktion* might be launched any day, and an *Aktion* meant certain death. On the other hand, there existed at least a possibility that our plan might succeed. It was of no avail. She wanted no part of any escape attempt.

Trying a different approach, I suggested that I go by myself, taking my daughter along with me. Still, I could not bear the thought of abandoning my mother with Pesachyah and his three children. On the other hand, I had to consider that all I would gain by remaining in the ghetto would be the doubtful privilege of being killed along with them when the Germans liquidated the ghetto. I had just about decided to leave, when Mother's sobbing, "Don't leave me! Don't leave me!" made me change my mind. I resolved to stay in the ghetto, placing my trust in the Almighty, Who would surely save us.

In Ghetto Two, one anxiety-filled day followed another as "extermination day" inexorably approached. During the daytime, I made the rounds of the streets of Ghetto One, trying to pick up news about the impending *Aktion*. The preparations for the *Aktion* were in the works. Only the date was still uncertain. While Ghetto Two was dormant and quiet, Ghetto One was bustling with activity; it was the marketplace for foreign documents which I still hoped to acquire. In the evenings, I returned to Ghetto Two to spend the night. Every morning I peered across the fence, fearful to find the ghetto surrounded by soldiers, which was the prelude to any *Aktion*.

One fateful night, the nightmare was upon us. Suddenly, tumultuous noise emerged from the city outside the ghetto. Although it was dark, I could detect a large contingent of German soldiers raising a commotion with their boisterous laughter. I was not particularly concerned, since they were assembled near the large barracks. Figuring that they had just arrived, or perhaps were ready to leave, I went back to sleep.

At the crack of dawn, one of our neighbors awoke me. He was shaking like a leaf.

"The ghetto is surrounded by German soldiers in full battle gear," he told me.

Since I already knew of the presence of soldiers in town, I did not pay much attention to him. But noting the people's growing anxiety, I soon became caught up in the general tense atmosphere. After all, if something was about to happen, we had to try to protect ourselves. I had not built a bunker, thinking that it would be worthless anyway, since the police knew the location of all the bunkers in the ghetto. Meanwhile, I awakened the family and told them to get dressed in a hurry.

The streets were now full of terror-crazed people. Scared stiff, they were scurrying in all directions, asking questions, getting no answers. A number of German guards entered the ghetto gate, walking around calmly, followed by other guards who entered from Ghetto One. Something's wrong here, I thought. I wonder what they have in mind? Ghetto One or Ghetto Two?

Mother approached the fence separating the two ghettos. She saw people carrying bundles. Where were they running? No answer. Everyone was preoccupied with himself. I suddenly noticed that in one lightning move the entire ghetto had been surrounded by soldiers manning machine guns, their barrels protruding through the boards of the fence. A few people were trying to run away, but the machine guns at the ready deterred them. This is the end, I thought.

Not wasting any time, I went home to lead everyone into the apartment of our neighbor who had a bunker. I didn't really believe it would be of any use, since the Jewish police had discovered it during the previous *Aktion*. Nonetheless, I had nothing better to offer, and the streets were absolutely unsafe. In my neighbor's apartment I met others who also knew of the existence of the bunker. I walked over to the bunker and opened the door.

"Listen, if you want to stay alive you'd better get in right away!" I called out. "Every minute counts. Remember, your life is at stake!"

A few people began to enter, when suddenly, a German monster appeared.

"*Alle heraus in den hof!*" he roared viciously. "Everybody out into the courtyard!"

Luckily, the German did not notice the open door of the bunker.

"*Jawohl, wir kommen sofort!*" we shouted back. "Okay, we're on our way!"

The German, relying on our assurance, continued on to the next apartment, hustling everyone out into the street.

Meanwhile, some of the men in our group decided to obey the order, laying in a supply of food in anticipation of a long journey. I urged the others to hurry into the bunker, but I waited a while before closing up the bunker, in case someone changed his mind and came back. Just then, in the very last minute, two of my brother Pesachyah's children appeared, a seven-year-old girl and a three-year-old boy, who had gotten lost in the confusion. Pesachyah and his third child never made it to the bunker and were placed on the death train. Neither did my little cousin who had been staying with us. I was the last one to enter the bunker, closing the latch from the inside.

The design of the bunker was quite unsophisticated, just a basic all-purpose bunker. In the corner of the dining room, an opening cut into the floor, measuring twenty inches by sixty inches, led into a room in the basement. The door leading to this basement room was bricked up, making it impossible to detect. The opening in the floor was covered with a rug on which a couch was placed. The last person to enter the bunker moved the couch over the hole—a complicated maneuver—but we managed somehow. The bunker had no window at all; it was pitch dark, and the air was stifling.

Surveying our bunker population, I found that there were thirteen of us, including my mother, my daughter, Pesachyah's two children and myself.

Since the courtyard of our building happened to be the central roundup point, large enough to hold the entire ghetto population, I requested that everyone be quiet so that we might hear what was going on outside. We could hear the terrifying howling and barking of the German beasts which always accompanied their *Aktionen*. The victims were loaded onto trucks amidst the bloodcurdling cries of the wailing and

shrieking women and children. We were sick at heart, overcome with grief, visualizing the horrifying fate awaiting our
innocent brothers and sisters. The crying lasted throughout
the night—until it became quiet. The trucks drove off, taking
their pathetic cargo to its final destination.

Staying in the bunker without light, air, toilet facilities
and, worst of all, without food, was quite distressing. In the
confusion, our people had forgotten to prepare a supply of
food. The adults and mature children understood that even
if there is no food you keep quiet. But my little girl Sheindl,
who wasn't quite three years old, would not take no for an
answer and began to cry for food. I did not know what to do,
until at last I found a bottle of water which I sweetened with
saccharin; that was her breakfast.

For a short while she kept quiet, and every time she cried,
we gave her some more of the sweet water. But we could not
hush her for very long. The water did not still her hunger
pangs, and her loud crying threatened to betray our hideout.
We decided to venture out to get the loaf of bread that had
been left on the dining room table. One of the girls, the
granddaughter of Rabbi Elimelech Zanger, was best suited to
get the bread; her father had not hidden out with us, since he
was convinced that the ghetto would not be annihilated. The
couch which covered the door to the bunker made it impossible to open it wide enough for an adult to pass through, but
the young girl could somehow manage to wiggle her way out
through the narrow space.

"If you run into a German, for Heaven's sake don't let on
that we are hiding in a bunker," we cautioned her. "Tell him
that you stowed away in a corner of the room."

She was an intelligent girl. We knew we could rely on her
not to give us away. Crawling on hands and knees to avoid

being seen from outside, she spotted a loaf of bread on the table. With a quick move, she grabbed it and hurried back into the bunker.

As soon as Sheindl's hunger was satisfied, she calmed down. The rest of the bread was set aside for her exclusively, for I did not know how long we would be holed up in the bunker.

And so we waited out the day. From outside came the silence of death. Not a soul stirred, not a sound was heard. We lingered on without a morsel of food or a drop of water—truly a fast day. We prayed for Hashem to have mercy on us.

CHAPTER 22

∎

In Search of Bunkers

F ROM THE START, IT SEEMED TO ME THAT THE *AKTION* did not extend into Ghetto One. Quite naively, I believed it was aimed only at Ghetto Two. My plan was, therefore, to move into Ghetto One now that Ghetto Two was finished, but a mountain of obstacles barred my way. First, how was I going to move across the fence separating the ghettos? The guard had been doubled in anticipation of people like myself emerging from their bunkers. Second, even if I were to make it into Ghetto One, where would I find a job and a place to stay? And most important, what was to happen to my mother and the small children?

At any rate, staying in the bunker was out. We were without food, water and air, not to mention the lack of sanitary facilities. But it was still too early to sneak across; the guards were still on the alert. Perhaps tomorrow night.

We spent that night in the bunker, our stomachs rumbling, our throats parched. One of us simply had to go out to try and find something to eat in one of the empty apartments. The job was given to Reich, a bright young man from Cracow who was equal to the task. We opened the door of the bunker, and Reich was on his way. It wasn't long before he returned from his expedition holding a few crusts of dry bread in one hand, the other hand carrying a bag filled with apples, carrots, beets and a jar of jelly.

He handed the food to me, and I saw to it that everything was divided fairly. Instead of distributing the entire harvest, I gave everyone, including the members of my family, just enough to stay alive, since no one could tell how long we would have to remain in the bunker. After this "satisfying" meal, we got ready to bed down on the hard, cold floor. The expectation that this would last only one more night kept our spirits up.

With Hashem's help, the night went by peacefully. The morning sun sent its soothing rays into a wounded world. A new day began, but instead of the hustle and bustle of laborers going to work, the ghetto was sheathed in a tomblike silence. We waited in vain for the workers from Ghetto One to bring us some news. Filled with gloom, I wondered, Who knows what happened to Ghetto One? Could they have been deported along with Ghetto Two? Then there was the worry of finding food. Otherwise, we'd all starve to death in this bunker! Dolefully, we stared at each other, filled with gloomy forebodings.

I simply have to find out what is going on in Ghetto One, I thought. I must make my way across somehow. Surely, I'll find some of my friends who will offer me shelter.

My mind was made up. I opened the door of the bunker, gingerly stepped over to my apartment and stuffed some clothes and underwear into a small valise. All the while, I was shaking like a leaf, since my apartment was only about ten feet away from the ghetto fence where the guards were keeping a close watch. I wanted to pack some food as well, but I could find nothing. I decided to return temporarily to the bunker.

Meanwhile, the other bunker dwellers, following my example, had gone to their homes and brought back all their possessions, bundles of clothing, linen and the like. I begged them to bring only the bare necessities, since there simply was no space in the small bunker, but they paid no attention to me. "It's a pity to leave it," was their answer. As a result of the overcrowding, life became even more unbearable than it was before.

Thank Heaven, that night in the bunker also passed without an incident. Towards mid-morning, we heard voices coming from the street. Reich, whom I instructed to reconnoiter, reported that it was a work detail doing some kind of work. We were glad to have evidence that at least Ghetto One had not been liquidated.

Back at the window, Reich recognized one of the laborers as a friend of ours. He called him over, but seeing Reich, the laborer raised his hands to his head.

"What, are you still here?" he cried out in horror. "Don't you know your life is in danger? You see, the Bochnia ghetto has been made *Judenrein*. The two ghettos have been liquidated. Most of the ghetto inmates were killed and burned on the spot, and the rest were hauled off to the extermination camps. From the five thousand Bochnia ghetto Jews only about two hundred laborers remain to remove the possessions the people left in their homes. When our job is done,

185

we too will be shipped off to some concentration camp."

The news shattered us. We realized that we were in mortal danger. Where could we go? How could we escape? Oblivious to hunger and thirst, all our thoughts focused on our perilous situation. It seemed hopeless. It would take a miracle to rescue us from this trap.

We sat in deadly silence, like on *Tishah b'Av*. Not a word was spoken. Suddenly, the silence was broken, the ghetto came alive. The shrill voices of bloodthirsty German demons mixed with the clatter of their hobnailed boots resounded through the streets, striking terror into our hearts. We heard them enter our building, hungrily searching for Jews who might be hiding out. I pressed my eye to a tiny crack in the bunker door to see what was going on. The Germans were moving from room to room, turning everything upside down, swinging hammers and hatchets, splitting walls, banging, cracking, breaking furniture, looking for bunkers.

I breathed a sigh of relief. Somehow, they had skipped the apartment that held our bunker. But then I saw the *Unterscharfuhrer* point at our apartment.

"Did you take care of this one?" he asked his men.

"*Jawohl*," came the reply.

"But did you smash it up?"

"No, not yet."

I was frozen with fear. We're done for, I thought. They're going to discover our bunker, no doubt about it. Over and over, I fervently prayed, *Ribono Shel Olam*, please save us from these accursed murderers!

"Let no one make a sound," I ordered. "Keep the children absolutely quiet."

The German monsters worked with great diligence, eager to perform the "*mitzvah*" of wiping out every last Jew. I heard them enter the room behind which our bunker was situated, camouflaged by a large clothes closet. After opening the closet door, they tried moving it. That's it! I thought. Yet I never abandoned faith and continuously prayed to Hashem to protect us.

"Stay calm," I whispered. "Keep quiet and don't move."

Just when we were ready to give up, Hashem performed the great miracle. As the Germans prepared to move the closet, one of them called out, "*Genug!* Enough! We have to move on!"

Seconds later, they were all gone, and we all drew long, deep breaths. Clearly, it was Hashem's indescribable miracle that had saved us from certain death. The experience lifted our spirits, filling us with gratitude to Hashem and renewed our faith in Him. We firmly believed that just as He had saved us in this instance, He surely would save us and release us from this living hell. With tear-filled eyes, we gazed silently at each other; our joy knew no bounds.

When our emotions subsided somewhat, the hunger pangs made themselves felt. After making sure that the streets were quiet and that the Germans had left, we sent one of our group to forage for some food. On his search, he ran into a Jewish policeman he knew, a man named Zimmet from Briegel, a nephew of Eliezer Landau. He told him about our group of thirteen people hiding in a bunker without a bite to eat for more than two days and asked him if he could provide us with some food. Zimmet, a good-hearted man from a *chassidic* background, promised to help us.

Towards evening, we heard a knock at the courtyard gate. Although we assumed it was Zimmet, we were afraid to open the gate which had been sealed by the Germans. Later that night, I sneaked outside to find a briefcase filled with bread and fruit, truly a self-sacrificing deed on Zimmet's part, one which could have cost him his life if the Germans had caught him. The sight of food brought big smiles to all faces; the long fast finally had come to an end.

The time had come to think about leaving the bunker. I planned to go by myself and mingle with the laborers. Since I still had my worker's overalls, I would blend in perfectly with the group. The greatest danger was the *Lagerfuhrer* who made a head count of the laborers twice a day, since he knew that scores of people hiding in bunkers would mingle with the workers. Whenever he would discover an unauthorized worker, he would shoot him on the spot without thinking twice. Knowing all his workers, he recognized the stowaways even before starting the head count. Many Jews fell victim to this inhuman creature.

What was I to do? I saw no option other than taking the risk. Ultimately, I wanted to escape from the ghetto, and I had to explore the possibilities for an escape route. Also, a way had to be found to supply food to the people in the bunker for the foreseeable future.

On *Shabbos*, I went out into the street and covertly slipped into the work detail. The workers were surprised to see me, wondering where I had come from. Convinced that I could trust them not to report me, I told them everything. Meanwhile, I learned that the Germans were constantly discovering new bunkers and immediately killed their occupants. It was estimated that there still were some five hundred people in various bunkers. With regard to finding an escape route, I did not make much headway, but I did manage to obtain a good supply of food for the bunker; both the workers and the Jewish policemen brought me all the food I needed.

CHAPTER 23

───────────■───────────

Escape from the Ghetto

R OUTINELY, I LEFT THE BUNKER EVERY DAY TO MINGLE
with the workers who kept me abreast of the latest
developments. I was careful to stay out of harm's
way, since the Gestapo and the *Lagerfuhrer* conducted daily
spot checks in order to make sure no infiltrators had joined
the work detail.

Walking the ghetto streets one day, I bumped into my
friend Herschel Kitover, who was hiding in a bunker with his
wife and child. Herschel was talking to another Jew, who was
also living underground, about ways of rescuing their families. Joining in the conversation, I suddenly recalled that I
owed Herschel a sum of money for some lace I had bought
from him. Herschel had given up hope of ever collecting the
money, thinking I had been killed or deported along with the

other Jews. As I pulled out my wallet to pay my debt, I was interrupted by Reb Yechezkel Halberstam, the son of the Rabbi of Bochnia, who just happened to pass.

"At a time like this, with life hanging in the balance, you still keep things like this in mind?" he burst out excitedly.

To me, it seemed a natural thing to do. Even while sitting in the bunker, I had complained to my mother that I regretted not having paid Herschel the money I owed him. Having met him now, I was only too happy to pay my debt.

As we were standing there, engaged in spirited conversation about possible escape plans, one of the bystanders suddenly called out, "*Oy vay!* We're finished!"

There he was, the *Lagerfuhrer* himself, one hundred feet away from us, escorted by his trained German shepherd police dog. This dog had shown his killer instinct during the last *Aktion* when, on his master's orders, he had ripped to pieces scores of Jews. And now we were standing face to face with this angel of death.

Quick as a flash, I picked myself up and started running toward the bunker. I had nothing to lose. If I stayed I would be torn apart by this dog. On the other hand, if I ran away there were two possibilities. One, the German might shoot me, but then there was the chance that he would miss, or hit me in a non-vital area. Two, he might send the dog after me; in that case, I would strangle the dog. When one's life is threatened, one finds sources of unknown strength.

The *Lagerfuhrer* was standing exactly opposite the house where our bunker was located. Fearful that he might see me enter the house, I quickly looked back to see if there was any reaction. All was quiet. No gunshots, no dog chasing me. To avoid being seen, I ran toward the rear of the house, climbed in through the window, knocked on the door of our bunker and hurriedly jumped inside. Not wishing to alarm the people in the bunker, I did not tell them about the incident, but the expression on my face gave me away. I had no choice but to tell them what had happened, but I tried to calm their fears. The minutes ticked away, and everything remained quiet.

Several hours later, I went out again. I had to find out what had happened to my two friends. I feared the worst since I had not seen them run away, but to my great surprise, there they were. They told me that when they saw me make a break for it, they too ran to find shelter in a nearby storage shed. The other fellow entered the shed in time, but Herschel did not make it, whereupon the *Lagerfuhrer* sent his dog after him. The dog ripped Herschel's pants to shreds, but when he offered no resistance, the dog left him alone to report his achievement to his master. Herschel, taking advantage of the respite, quickly slipped into the storage shed, where the German never found him. Thus, the three of us were saved by what was undeniably a clear-cut divine miracle.

This incident brought home to me most vividly that I had no option but to attempt to escape from the ghetto. It was only a matter of time before the Germans would discover our bunker, just as they had unearthed all the other bunkers. Too many people knew about our hideaway, a fact which made our stay riskier by the day.

I now thought back once again to the Jewish organization in Prokatzim near Cracow which smuggled people across the Polish-Slovak border, from where they made their way to Hungary, and I again considered the possibility of using their services as an avenue of escape. However, before I could dream of crossing the border, I had to get out of the ghetto, which at that time was heavily guarded. Besides, I was not alone, and having to take along my mother and the children made any escape attempt all the more difficult.

Pondering the problem, I came up with a plan. Since the Jewish policemen were generally on very good terms with their Polish counterparts, I asked Zimmet, the Jewish policeman who had provided us with food, to put me in touch with a reliable Polish policeman. He took care of it at once, and he pointed out to me the policeman with whom he had arranged a meeting.

Speaking of Zimmet, I want to point out that this gallant Jewish policeman risked his life for us many times. While we were in the bunker, he kept us from starving. Every night, at great personal risk, he filled a bag with food he collected from empty Jewish homes and pushed it through a break in the main door. Even now, arranging the meeting with the Polish policeman was fraught with grave danger, since any contact between Jewish and Polish policemen was punishable by death. Ultimately, his life ended in tragedy when he helped an entire Jewish family escape from the ghetto. They were caught, and under agonizing German torture, they revealed the identity of their benefactor. The Gestapo, true to form, shot and killed the valiant Zimmet.

Without waiting, I approached the Pole, but fearful of being caught conversing to me, he directed me to wait for him in a hidden corner. When we met, I came straight to the point.

"Look here, I want to escape from the ghetto," I said without mincing words. "I want you to help me by escorting me to Cracow, or at least to Prokatzim."

I reasoned that under official police escort my trip would be safer. No one would question me, since they would assume I had been arrested and was being taken to Cracow for interrogation. I promised the Pole a beautiful piece of worsted wool cloth for a suit and one hundred *zlotys* in cash for his cooperation.

"I'm sorry," the Pole replied. "Escorting you to Cracow, or anywhere else for that matter, is out of the question. Ever since the *Aktion*, the Germans don't even allow us to go home. They're afraid we'll steal things from the Jewish homes. But I'm willing to help you get out of the ghetto. Anyway, I can't do it tonight, because I'm off duty. It'll just have to wait till Thursday."

We agreed to meet at nine o'clock in the evening on Thursday. Before that hour, it would not be dark yet, and after nine, it would be too difficult to leave the ghetto, since the guard would be reinforced.

I returned to the bunker, hoping that with Hashem's help things would work out. Mother, too, was overjoyed to be able to leave this living hell. Hoping to save the lives of the other bunker residents, I informed everyone about my plan, telling them to meet the Polish policeman at the time and the place I had arranged with him. But man proposes, and the Lord disposes.

The *Lagerfuhrer* turned out to be not only a rabid Jew-hater but a shrewd and cunning fox as well. At first, he seemed to ignore the hundreds of people hiding out in bunkers. He reasoned that the bunker residents, seeing they were being left alone, would become careless and reveal their hiding places. Thus, it was fully a week after the *Aktion*, when the police had already discovered most of the bunkers, when he ordered the police to fan out over the two ghettos and arrest all the remaining bunker occupants.

On Wednesday night, the night the command was issued, we did not have the slightest inkling that anything was afoot.

We were packing our meager possessions in anticipation of our departure the following night. I placed some clothes, underwear and food into a small valise and wrapped the material for the Polish policeman in a separate package. I also prepared a business suit for myself, since wearing overalls would mark me as a ghetto inmate.

A bright moon illuminated the star-studded sky, reminding me that I had not yet recited *Kiddush Levanah*, the Sanctification of the New Moon. Mindful that *Sefer Chassidim* assures us that no evil will befall us during any month in which we recite *Kiddush Levanah*, Reich and I and another man left the bunker to recite this prayer under the open sky which is where it preferably should be said. Because of the late hour, we did not want to venture out into the street. Instead, we said the prayer quietly in the room facing the street. The words lifted our spirits and strengthened our faith that the Almighty would rescue us.

Back in the bunker, I shaved so as not to arouse suspicion, since according to the plan I was to travel as an Aryan. This was going to be our last night in the bunker. Who could know what tomorrow would bring?

After a tense night we got up very early, impatiently awaiting the moment when at long last the ghetto walls would disappear behind us. At the same time, we were apprehensive, fearful of the unknown. In our hearts, we knew that only a miracle could save us.

After breakfast, as usual, I went out into the street to find out the latest developments. Hardly did I emerge from the front door when Yosef Sternhell, a young man I knew from Cracow, came over to me to hand me an important message from a policeman whom I knew since childhood and who used to *daven* with me in the same *shtiebel*.

"You should know," the message read, "that we received orders to search for bunkers. Be prepared to take action before it is too late!"

I felt as though someone had struck me over the head with a hammer. Just now, in the last moment, when salvation seemed so near, all was lost. I tried to think of a way out, but down the street I saw them coming—a police unit about to start the raid. The search for bunkers was under way. There was no time left for any plans.

A thought flashed through my mind. I realized there was no way to save my mother, who would not abandon her small grandchildren, but I hoped to save at least my daughter and myself. I ran to the bunker, and with the excuse that I had found warm water and wanted to give her a bath, I called down to my mother to hand me my daughter quickly. The child was still asleep.

"Hurry up! Hurry up!" I called urgently. "Hand me Sheindl! Make it quick!"

My mother could not understand my impatience, but I saw no point in revealing the imminent danger. I had not yet figured out what I was going to do. One thing was uppermost in my mind. I had to get away as fast as I could. They would arrive any minute now.

By the time I was finally carrying the child in my arms, ready to run from the house, ten policemen blocked my exit. I tried to force my way out, but one of them, a fellow who happened to be an old acquaintance of mine (I won't mention his name out of respect for his father who was a decent and upright man), stopped me.

"Hold it right there, Friedman!" he yelled. "Where do you think you're going?"

In sheer desperation, I broke through the tight circle of

policemen and ran toward Horowitz, the deputy chief of the *Judenrat*, who was in charge of the raid.

"Mr. Horowitz, please have mercy on me and my little baby," I pleaded.

Horowitz was surprised to see me carrying a child in my arms. I had asked my mother to wrap her tightly in a blanket, making it appear as though I was carrying a package. If the German guards would have seen me carrying a child they would have killed both of us instantly.

"How come you're in the ghetto?" Horowitz asked. "Aren't you supposed to be with the workers?"

"You are quite right," I replied, "but my child got sick, so I came into the ghetto last night to be with her. I'm begging you, please let me go. I promise you that tonight I'm leaving the ghetto. I've made arrangements with a Polish policeman."

"You trust a Pole?" Horowitz asked, giving me a quizzical look. "He'll take everything he can get out of you, and in the end, he'll hand you over to the SS."

"What do you care?" I answered. "Look, if you don't want to give me an official release, just look the other way and let me get away."

Seeing me conferring with the chief, the policemen relied on him to do his job and continued their house-to-house search. Meanwhile, several workers who were watching me plead with Horowitz urged him to let me go. He turned around, and I ran.

From the distance, I could see the unfortunate people being led out of the bunker, including my mother and her small grandchildren. I was heartbroken and overcome with grief. What could I do? I was in mortal danger myself. Mother was marched off by the police, while I walked in the opposite direction toward the safety of Herschel Kitover's bunker.

The entrance leading to his bunker was very difficult to find, and because of the darkness, I tripped and fell into a deep hole. I was bruised pretty badly, but thank Heaven, my child was not hurt. Before long I heard the cries of the policemen.

"*Yidden, Yidden,* come out of your bunkers!" they coaxed. "Nothing bad will happen to you!"

Over and over, they repeated their call, but I kept quiet. Distrustful, they searched feverishly, shining their flashlights into every corner—until they discovered me and my daughter. Breaking out in a cold sweat, I tried to convince them to ignore me.

"You all saw that Horowitz let me go," I said, my voice cracking with fear.

After conferring with each other, one of them said, "Okay, we'll let you stay, but you've got to tell us if there are other people hidden here."

"There's no one else," I said. "You can go and see for yourself. There is absolutely no room for anyone besides myself."

This seemed to satisfy them, and they went away.

I took a deep breath. I had saved my own life and that of Herschel, his wife and child. I then asked Herschel to open the bunker, whereupon he invited me and my child to stay with them.

Herschel's bunker was a simple structure. They had built a dummy brick wall in the cellar, leaving a small opening for an entrance which could be closed from the inside. The bunker was so low that one could only sit on the floor. They had sufficient food and candles, and since I had not eaten all day, the bread they offered me revived me.

After the events of the day, all I had left was the overalls I was wearing. I knew that trying to leave the ghetto in this outfit would be impossible. Besides, I had also been forced to abandon the piece of material for the Polish policeman; it would be very unwise to go meet him without this material, since in his anger he was liable to hand me over to the Gestapo. I decided to go back to our old bunker to change into my business suit and retrieve the material.

Leaving the child with Herschel, I went out into the street. The laborers I met told me that the raid on the bunkers had ended with the capture of a large number of people. Entering our bunker, I found everything in terrible disarray. After leading away the occupants, the Jewish policemen came back to ransack and loot the bunker, taking anything of value, silver, gold, diamonds and good clothing which had been abandoned by the deportees. These men were living under the illusion that they were safe and secure, not realizing that only a few days after they led the bunker people to their deaths, the same fate would befall them. Indeed, after the liquidation of the ghetto, all remaining Jews—a total of two hundred and seventy persons—including the *Judenrat* and the Jewish police were carried off to the Tchebno death camp, where only a small percentage survived.

Rummaging through the clutter, I could not find the suit that I had prepared for myself, and I had to make do with another suit. Luckily, I did find the material and brought everything to the new bunker, including some food that I stumbled on.

I went back into the street to find a way to send a good-bye letter to my poor mother who was imprisoned in the basement of the Judenrat, awaiting her fate. I wrote with a trembling hand.

A brievele tzu die mame (a letter to mother)

Dear Mother,

Please don't worry too much about your present situation. We have done all we could do. I intend to flee the ghetto tonight, along with my daughter. Pray that our journey to Hungary be successful and that we arrive there safely, so that at least one member of our entire family will survive. Be strong and of good cheer.

Your only son

I sent the letter through Reb Yechezkel Halberstam, the son of the Rabbi of Bochnia, who worked in the labor detail.

After saying good-bye to all my friends and acquaintances, I returned to the bunker, changed my clothes and waited impatiently for nine o'clock, the hour of my appointment with the Polish policeman. My friend Herschel tried to dissuade me from going through with my plan, arguing that it was too dangerous. He suggested that I stay with him, assuring me that he had enough food to last for several days.

I turned down his offer. "And what are we going to do a few days from now when the food runs out?" I told him. "In the end, we'll have to get out of the ghetto anyway, so isn't it a pity to pass up a golden opportunity like this?"

Impressed by my argument, he began to ponder the merits of joining me, but it took a long time for him to make up his mind. By the time he decided to come along with me, he confessed that in order to gain time he had set the clock back by one hour and that it was actually ten o'clock already.

I was terribly upset. Would the Pole still be waiting? Aside from that, by this time the guard would be doubled, making it much more difficult to leave the ghetto. Nonetheless, since I had decided that this was to be the night, I did not want to postpone it. We decided to go.

Gingerly, we emerged from the bunker, careful not to make the slightest sound. The place where we were to meet the policeman was a good distance away. The bright light of the full moon combined with the flames of a huge bonfire to illuminate the ghetto. The fire, which had been set by the Germans, was consuming *Sifrei Torah* and other *sefarim* in a blazing inferno. Crawling on hands and knees, we made our way furtively to the meeting place where, much to my surprise, we found a group of around fifteen people waiting. Evidently, word of my plan of escape had leaked out, and they all wanted to join me.

It certainly placed the whole project at risk; the presence of a large group of people in a ghetto street at this late hour was bound to arouse suspicion and jeopardize the entire escape attempt. Nevertheless, I said nothing; perhaps it would work anyway.

We waited and waited, but no Polish policeman appeared. He had probably left when I did not show up at nine o'clock. Carrying my little girl in my arms, I went looking for him, but I soon gave up and returned to the group. We sized up the situation and decided to try to sneak out of the ghetto on our own. One of the boards of the fence was quickly pulled out, and one after another we slid through the narrow opening.

Just when we all made it through the fence and took a few steps, a volley of rifle shots rang out behind us. Everyone ran forward in a mad dash, thinking that ahead lay the free streets of the city. Instead, we ran head-on into a barbed wire barricade that was invisible in the dark. Cries of pain erupted, especially from the children. My little girl, whom I was carrying in my arms, also broke out crying; only later did I notice that her entire head was full of cuts and bruises. The situation was desperate. The cries would surely give us away, and they'd catch up with us.

Instantly, I took cover, lying down flat on the ground, hiding in the tall grass. I begged Sheindl to keep quiet; somehow, she understood and stifled her whimpering. For a long time, I lay there without moving a muscle.

It's all over, I thought. But then I regained confidence. Don't give up hope, I told myself. Place your faith in Hashem; strengthen yourself, and He will give you strength.

Most of the people made it into the courtyard of a house, hoping to go out into the Polish part of town. The Pole who lived in the house, alerted by the noise outside, came out.

"Hey, you Jews!" he roared. "Get back into the ghetto! Police! Police!"

The situation was critical. It would be foolish to stay in the grass any longer; the Germans would undoubtedly find me when they combed the area. I had to get out!

I jerked myself off the ground. Crouching low, I moved away from the danger zone. Then I ran for my life.

Running along the barricade, I noticed a small section made up of a brick wall, low enough for me to climb over. At the same time, peering into the dark, I made out the dark silhouette of a figure standing on the other side of the wall. I saw no way to climb the wall while carrying my child, and I stood there for a moment pondering my predicament. Suddenly, a pair of hands emerged from the other side, reaching out toward me. Without a moment's hesitation, I handed the child to him, climbed the wall and took the child back from the mysterious, shadowy man.

Herschel, who had been following me, then thrust his child into my hands. Then he and his wife climbed across the wall, so that we were all standing in the free part of town. I turned to thank the mysterious stranger who had so graciously helped us, but to my utter surprise, he had vanished into nothingness without leaving a trace. To this day, I wonder who it was. In my heart, I believe it was a *malach* sent by Hashem to save us.

We quickened our pace to get away as far as possible from the ghetto. Suddenly, we heard the sound of gunfire at close range. We realized the gunfire was directed at the group that had been betrayed by the Pole. Since then, I have never seen or heard of any of them again; evidently, they were all killed.

As to my two partners at the *Kiddush Levanah* of the previous night, they just happened to be out in the street when the police discovered our bunker. After hiding out in various places, they managed an amazing escape by breaking through the ghetto wall in broad daylight. I do not know what happened to them afterwards.

CHAPTER 24

■

Alone on the Road

THE MARCH I HAD MADE FROM BOCHNIA TO DOMIENITZ a short time before—when I was drafted to work in the Domienitz forest and was forced, on the first day, to walk the entire distance on foot—now stood me in good stead.

Boarding a train in Bochnia would be hazardous, as the station had been heavily guarded since the first *Aktion*. We had no choice but to walk all the way to Domienitz and catch the train to Cracow from there. We set out on our march, having in mind to spend the night somewhere near the Domienitz station, so as to catch the first train in the morning. This train was never checked, since it was always crammed with laborers on their way to work. Besides, we reasoned, no one would take notice of us in the early morning darkness.

A few minutes into our march, we suddenly noticed two SS men in full regalia strutting toward us.

"I know them," whispered Herschel. "They are Beck and Bogusch, the two worst bloodhounds of the ghetto."

We were proceeding straight ahead, while the Germans were approaching from a side street, so that we would meet at the intersection, a highly distasteful prospect, to say the least. Herschel dashed ahead in order to reach the intersection before the Germans did, but I did not follow suit, thinking that a large group on the run would arouse suspicion. Instead, I stayed in place and waited for them to cross the street and continue on their way. To my disappointment, they turned right, proceeding on a collision course with me. Taking cover behind a small stairwell, I watched with apprehension as the two SS men approached in my direction. In spite of my Polish appearance, it was not hard to figure out that I was a Jew escaping from the ghetto. Carrying a child and a small valise in Bochnia, within a short distance from the ghetto, gave me all the earmarks of a ghetto escapee.

Suddenly, their bright flashlights were shining into my face.

"Where are you going?" they asked, pointing at my valise. "Did you arrive at the station just now?"

"No, I'm going *to* the station," I replied, petrified with fear.

I instantly realized I had made two mistakes. First, I should have answered I had indeed come *from* the station, since the last train had already left a long time before. My second mistake was speaking to them in German, a telltale sign that I was a Jew since Poles rarely speak German.

The Germans looked at each other with raised eyebrows, as if to say, "There's something strange about this fellow."

Without waiting for further questions I bolted toward the station.

"Maybe I'll still catch the train!" I shouted, running as fast as I could.

Miraculously, they did not order me to come back, nor did they shoot at me. I do not know what got into them at that particular moment. I am convinced it was Hashem's protective Hand shielding me. When Herschel noticed that I had been stopped by the two SS men he quickly ran away. I did not find him any more.

In the dark, I could not find the road leading to Domienitz, and I was forced to ask directions from a Pole. In an attempt to make my nocturnal walk with a child in my arms look more plausible, I placed a bandage on Sheindl's head. No one will suspect me now, I thought. The first Pole I asked for directions to the Domienitz station eyed me with suspicion.

"Get away from me," he snarled. "I know you're a Jew. Don't give me any stories. You're running away from the ghetto."

Happy that the Pole let it go at that and did not alert the police, I continued on my way. The next Pole I asked for directions gave me an entirely different answer. He, too, recognized that I was a Jew.

"My friend," he said, "you did the right thing escaping from the ghetto. Don't worry. The political situation is getting better by the day. Go into hiding until the war is over. It won't last much longer." He paused briefly. "In the village down the road you'll find many policemen patrolling the streets. Don't pay any attention to them; just walk down Main Street without fear. You'll also notice many people sitting in front of their homes. Don't worry about them either."

I wanted to thank the kindhearted man, but before I

could say anything, he vanished. I was not sure if he was a Pole or perhaps even a Jew. To my mind, he was another heavenly messenger sent by Hashem to save me.

Before long, I had evidence of the soundness of his advice. All along the main street, peasants were sitting outside enjoying the cool evening breeze. If the kind Pole had not guided me I would have been afraid to pass through the hamlet in full view of the policemen and the local peasants.

After a while, I reached a fork in the road. Should I turn to the right or to the left? It was already late, the road was deserted, and there was no one to ask. The best thing, it seemed, was to spend the night right there and continue on in the morning. The soft grass was my bed. My coat and the material I had prepared for the Polish policeman served as a blanket for my little girl, while I shivered throughout the night.

The hours passed with agonizing slowness. In the distance, I heard the chimes of the Bochnia bell tower tolling the hours. At last, dawn was breaking, the farm workers' heavy boots were pounding the gravel as they marched off to work.

"Which way to Domienitz?" I inquired of a worker.

The worker told me how to get there, but at the same time I realized I had missed the early morning train which took the workers to Cracow. I had no choice but to hire a horse-drawn wagon. However, since it was Friday, the market day in Bochnia, everyone was going *to* Bochnia. Finally, I found a peasant who agreed to take me, demanding the unheard of sum of three hundred *zlotys*. Without haggling, I agreed to pay the full amount, which made him suspicious of the entire deal.

"The next train is leaving in an hour," he said, scrutinizing me. "Why don't you go by train?"

"Don't you see?" I replied. "My little girl is hurt. I've got to get her to a doctor, and she's afraid to ride the train."

"Do you take me for a fool?" he snapped. "I know perfectly well what you're trying to do . . . but I'll take you anyhow." Evidently, the easy money influenced his decision.

I mounted the wagon with my daughter, and he returned to the village to have a bite to eat and feed the horse. Meanwhile, I warmed up a little from the cold night, and Sheindl drank a cup of fresh warm milk, something she had not had in a long time. The Pole then told me that he did not have time to take me, but that his thirteen-year-old son would drive the wagon. Furthermore, the boy could only take us as far as Niepolomitz, midway to Cracow, because he needed the wagon. This was clearly just a lame excuse. The truth was that he was afraid to risk his life transporting Jews, whereas his son, being a minor, would go free if caught. Instead of the three hundred *zlotys*, however, he offered to charge me only two hundred *zlotys*. Since I had no alternative, I accepted his proposal, thinking, When I get to Niepolomitz I'll worry about continuing my trip.

At last, the wagon was ready. I sat down on the floor, keeping the child next to me as the wagon rolled along the main highway. Buses, cars and trucks manned by German police and Gestapo whizzed past us, and I could not help but feel that every German had his eyes on me.

At one o'clock in the afternoon, we reached our destination. The boy stopped the wagon at the outskirts of Niepolomitz, evidently on his father's orders. After I paid him, he turned the wagon around and left.

I found myself at the side of the highway, fully exposed to the passing German vehicles. Putting Sheindl to sleep in the grass, I set out to find another wagon to take us to Cracow.

Suddenly, from the distance I heard someone shouting, "Hey you! Come over here!"

My heart skipped a beat. The stranger had probably guessed I was a Jew. But I simply had to go. Otherwise, he might shoot me.

"What are you looking for?" he asked.

"I'm looking for a wagon to take me and my sick child to Cracow to see a doctor," I answered calmly.

"Let me warn you that this is a very unsafe area," the man cautioned me. "Get off this highway, if you know what's good for you. Down the road is Gestapo Headquarters. The area is crawling with SS men. You'll never catch a ride around here anyhow. You're better off following the country roads all the way to Cracow. That way you won't run into any Germans."

He explained to me exactly how to go, accompanying me part of the way. Gratefully, I gave him a tip for his kind advice and continued in the direction he had indicated. I am convinced that this too was a miracle from Heaven; it was the third time a mysterious stranger had come along to save my life.

At first, trudging along the country trails was easy enough, but carrying my child in the midday sun took its toll and forced me to stop at a farmhouse to ask for a drink of water. The kind farmer offered me a cool drink; I washed my hands for *netillas yadayim* and ate a breakfast consisting of a piece of dry bread and a cup of water. Refreshed and invigorated, I continued my march, but since I did not know the way well, I decided to follow the railroad tracks.

Walking in total silence, I did not encounter a soul all day, but once, passing a field, I heard the field workers shout, "*Zhid! Zhid!* Jew! Jew!"

When I saw them in the distance, I pondered whether to

say hello to them in the traditional Polish greeting of "The Lord bless you." But I decided to look the other way, so as not to attract their attention. Although they had apparently concluded that I was a Jew, since there were no Germans around I was not afraid they would report me.

Parched after hours of walking in the blazing sun through the monotonous countryside I came upon a little pond. The water was covered with algae, pond weeds and frogs croaking happily. It did not matter; it was water. Using my cap as a cup, I first gave a drink to little Sheindl who had all along been moaning, "I'm so thirsty!" Then I quenched my own thirst. Refreshed, I resumed the long trek. But before long, we were thirsty again, and this time I could not even find a muddy puddle to moisten our dried lips.

Towards evening, as the sun slowly descended, I noticed in the distance a lonely cluster of trees reaching up from amidst the placid fields. Dragging myself to the small oasis with my last ounce of strength, I sat down on a stump to rest in the cool shade. It was a perfect place to *daven*. I took out my *tallis* and *tefillin* and immersed myself in *tefillah*. No one would find me here. After *davening*, I took out a slice of bread, and Sheindl and I enjoyed the meal.

But what good is a meal without a drink of water? I began to search, hoping that in the *zchus* of the innocent little one, Hashem would grant me a miracle of finding water. And indeed, after only a few minutes, I heard the sound of water bubbling up from the ground. There it was—a spring of pure clear water rising from the earth. I filled my cap with the cool life-giving water, slaking Sheindl's thirst and my own. The sense that Hashem was manifestly watching over us imbued me with hope and courage. With renewed vitality, I resumed the march.

Slowly, the long shadows of the night enveloped all of existence. I did not have the foggiest notion of where I was or how far I was from my destination of Cracow and Prokatzim. In the far-off distance, I detected a work detail digging a ditch. Should I go over and ask for directions? If they were Poles, they might hand me over to the Germans, and if they were Jewish laborers, no doubt they were being watched by German guards. Either way, I would be risking my life. In the end, I decided to approach them, placing my trust in Hashem. He had helped me thus far. He would help me again.

Coming closer, I noticed that they were Jews. Yet strangely, they were working without any supervision—a very rare occurrence indeed. I approached and asked them for directions to Cracow.

"Where are you from, and where are you headed?" they answered with a question, in typically Jewish fashion.

Briefly, I told them my story, explaining that I was trying to get to Cracow, but I did not tell them I intended to flee across the border and go to Hungary; such things are better left unsaid. However, instead of giving me the information I required, they tried to convince me to give up my plans of going to Cracow and Prokatzim, for my chances of survival would be very slim. They were willing—as a favor—to allow me to join them in their labor camp along with my daughter.

"You know, there are no children in this camp," they told me. "The Germans killed all children before carting off their parents to labor camps. But the Jewish camp doctor has influence with the *Lagerfuhrer*. He can arrange to have her stay with you."

Before I had a chance to answer, one of the men called out, "Quick, someone go get the doctor!"

Having experienced the comforts of life in a German

labor camp, I politely but firmly rejected their offer. These poor Jews still harbored the illusion that by working in a labor camp they would survive the war. I knew better.

"If that's your decision, you'd better leave in a hurry before the German guard arrives," one of the men said. "If he sees you, you're doomed. You're not too far from Cracow, but you've got to be very careful. At this hour of the evening, all the forced laborers are returning from work guarded by SS men who are itching for a chance to blow a Jew to bits."

Heeding their advice, I proceeded cautiously, and with Hashem's help, I made it safely to the railroad station. I wanted very much to go by train, yet at the same time I was afraid of being asked to show identification papers, which I did not have. Then again, I was so tired from marching all day that I was ready to collapse. In the end, I decided to throw caution to the winds and go by train as far as Prokatzim. After a long wait, I finally saw the train pull into the station. Assuming a nonchalant air, I quickly bought my ticket, seemingly indifferent to the bystanders who were gazing with curious stares at the little girl I was carrying in my arms.

I hurriedly boarded the train, and we were on our way. Our railroad car had no light. It was pitch-dark; one couldn't see a thing. Still, to be on the safe side, I stayed in the hallway.

"Prokatzim!" the conductor announced after a short ride.

I was elated, especially considering that walking this distance would have taken me several hours. The train came to a halt. Getting off, I bypassed the crush at the main exit hall and took a shortcut into town.

Thank Heaven, I had made it!

CHAPTER 25

∎

The Rescue Committee

P ROKATZIM! I HAD REACHED MY DESTINATION, BUT I DID not have the faintest notion of how to find the organizers of the escape route to Hungary. Since these people were living under assumed Aryan names, I had no way of identifying them.

It was already quite late. The nine o'clock curfew was approaching, the streets would be deserted, and I had nowhere to turn. Weighing the alternative options, I took the calculated risk of asking one of the men I had seen on the train whether he knew of any people in Prokatzim who held foreign citizenship. My question could have landed me in deep trouble, but to my surprise, it did not.

"Why, certainly. Not far from here, there lives a Jew who owns foreign citizenship papers," was the man's amazing reply. "I'll be happy to take you to his house."

Overjoyed at his cordial attitude, I saw his answer as yet another sign from Heaven that Hashem was guiding my footsteps and preventing me from stumbling into any pitfalls. We got into a friendly chat; the man apparently thought that I, too, was a foreign citizen, and I certainly did nothing to make him think otherwise. When we reached the house, I thanked him wholeheartedly, and flashing a warm smile, he bid me good-bye.

I rang the bell, and after a moment a Polish maid came to the door.

"What do you want?" she asked brusquely.

"I arrived in town just a short while ago, and I don't have a place to stay," I explained. "Could I just lie down to sleep in a corner of the house?"

Through the glass door, I could see her convey my request to the master of the house. She returned at once.

"Impossible," she said curtly. "You can't stay here."

"Don't you see?" I tried to reason with her. "It's late already, and I'm not allowed to stay in the streets. All I'm asking is to sleep in the hall. In the morning, I'll be on my way."

Suddenly, the master of the house emerged.

"Get out of here," he shouted. "There are no Jews living in this house. Beat it! Get lost!"

The uproar he created could be heard clear across town. All I needed was for the police to respond to the ruckus. That would be the last straw. After he calmed down a bit, I held up Sheindl.

"Look at the little girl in my arms," I pleaded. "What am I supposed to do? I have no place to go at this hour of the night. I know you are Jewish. Have a heart! Take pity on the little one! All I'm asking for is a small corner in which to spend the night."

"No," he insisted. "I'm not Jewish, and if you don't leave this minute I'm going to call the police!"

When he saw me stall for time, he started screaming at the top of his voice, "Police! Police!"

I begged him to stop screaming, and he finally calmed down and went back into the house. I found myself out in the street facing a grave predicament. I had nowhere to turn.

So I won't get any sleep, I thought to myself, but my little girl hasn't had a bite to eat or a drink of water for many hours. I decided to knock on another door of the house. Once again, the maid answered the door. When she heard that I wanted a drink of water, she went back into the house and did not return. After waiting a good while, I knocked again, this time on the window. No reaction at all. But I was not about to give up. The crying and moaning of the thirsty child might alert a policeman, and that would be real trouble.

I was furious.

"How can a Jew be so heartless?" I lashed out angrily. "You ought to be ashamed of yourselves, denying a Jew a drink of water! Don't you have any compassion?"

Presently, the master of the house came to the door.

"There's a well in the courtyard," he told me without opening the door. "Take as much water as you want."

After placing Sheindl on the floor, I went to look for the well, but I was unable find it in the dark. I returned to the front door.

"Sir, I can't find the well!" I called out.

"Just keep looking," he replied blandly.

Once more I searched, but still, I could find no sign of a well. Again, I begged him to give me just a cup of water, but the callous, good-for-nothing just turned a deaf ear.

In spite of everything, I did not forget that it was Friday night. Hiding in a corner, I *davened Kabbalas Shabbos* and sang *zemiros*. Since I had no water to wash my hands for *netillas yadayim*, I was unable to recite the *Kiddush* and eat bread. I could do without it, but little Sheindl kept moaning, "Water, water!" Seeing the child suffer was sheer torture.

"In the morning I'll get you water," I said, trying to appease her.

I prepared a bed for her in the grass, lulling her asleep with the promise of water and food in the morning.

No more than half an hour had gone by when, wonder of wonders, a window was opened, and through it a lady gently lowered a basket containing hot coffee and food. Sheindl did not want to touch the food, but she eagerly drank the entire cup. Because of concern regarding *kashrus*, I did not want to eat the food. I thanked the lady and explained this to her, asking her to take the food back, but to let me have just some water. Seconds later, she lowered a bottle of water from the window. After washing my hands, I recited the *Kiddush* over bread instead of wine and sang to myself the *zemiros,* sitting on the ground at my make-believe, open-air *Shabbos* meal.

It began to rain as soon as I fell asleep. I found shelter underneath a narrow porch among coils of barbed wire that were stored there. Just as I began to stretch out, the maid appeared with a blanket which I wrapped around Sheindl, making a comfortable bed for her. My body was aching all over, but at least the little one was sleeping soundly.

At the crack of dawn, the maid came to make sure I had not made off with the blanket. Returning a short time later, she invited us in. Imagine my surprise when the man of the house smilingly invited me to join him for a breakfast of fresh buttered rolls and piping hot coffee. At the same time, he apologized for his cold-hearted conduct the night before.

"I am not really a callous person," he said. "But a few days ago, there was a big robbery at the home of a friend of mine—also a foreign national—and since I didn't know you, I was afraid you had foul play in mind."

I thanked him, and then he inquired about my situation.

"Don't worry," he reassured me. "I know the people who are helping Jews escape to Hungary. I'll be glad to introduce you to them."

Patiently, he waited for my little girl to finish her meal, after which he took me to the house of the escape organization. To avoid being associated with me, he asked me to follow him at a distance. After we had walked for a good while, he pointed out the house. I thanked him for his kindness, and we parted.

Upon entering the house, I was met by two men I knew from Cracow and Bochnia, who were now officials on the rescue committee. However, my hopes of receiving a friendly reception from these old acquaintances were promptly dashed when the two men showed me the door and sent me packing. I was deeply hurt. They knew what I had been through, and instead of inquiring if my little girl needed some food or drink—never mind asking if I was hungry—they threw me out into the street. Meanwhile, they were seated around a table richly laden with an abundance of fish, meat, *challos* and other delicacies. Only people with hearts of stone could act like this; it was incomprehensible. I implored them to help me.

"I have money," I assured them. "I can pay."

It was useless.

"Look here, you had better get going," they answered

with grim finality. "There's nothing to discuss."

They directed me to the home of the Stern brothers, who were also foreign nationals.

"They'll take care of you," they said.

Thankfully, the Stern brothers offered me a warm welcome. After *davening Shacharis*, they invited me to a sumptuous *Shabbos* meal. It wouldn't be bad at all if I could stay here until I continue my journey, I thought. But I was in for a letdown when one of the brothers approached me.

"Reb Yid, please forgive us," he said apologetically. "We must ask you to leave at once. We are scheduled to leave for Hungary today, and the apartment will be returned to our Polish landlord."

What was I to do? I picked up my child and my valise and left together with the Stern brothers. They escorted me to the home of Reb Yitzchak Glanzer, the pre-war *shochet* of Cracow and Padgursz.

Reb Yitzchak Glanzer, an old friend of mine, received me with obvious delight. Much to my surprise, I met there my friend Herschel Kitover with his wife and child who had become separated from me when we ran into the two SS men shortly after escaping from the Bochnia ghetto. They, too, had suffered a great deal before reaching Prokatzim. I was very happy to see they had made it to safety and gratified that I had been instrumental in their rescue. Reb Yitzchak Glanzer did not keep us waiting. Within minutes, he set the table and produced a feast that was nothing short of a royal banquet.

After the meal, we sat down to some serious talk. Here I was, a fugitive without any papers, liable to be picked up in the first dragnet.

"I must leave as soon as possible," I said gravely.

"I'm willing to do all I can to help you," Reb Yitzchak

replied. "I'm slated to cross the border into Slovakia today, but I'm going to give up my seat on the transport and let you go instead."

His noble and unselfish offer brought tears to my eyes. He immediately informed the officers of the escape committee, who approved the switch; his trip would be postponed until the next opportunity. Meanwhile, I enjoyed Reb Yitzchak's hospitality, which knew no bounds. He even offered me his own bed while he slept on the floor. It was my first restful moment in the ten days since the beginning of the Bochnia *Aktion*.

Although the escape committee had agreed to the substitution, they went back on their word and refused to include me in the transport. Day after day, I urged them to let me go, pointing out that the local police knew all foreign nationals and any new face would arouse suspicion. They persistently refused with the justification that both I and my daughter looked Jewish and, since we had to make the trip to the border as non-Jews, our appearance would give us away. It was a flimsy excuse, since many Jews fled daily across the border without any trouble. The committee's true motive for turning me down was sheer greed. Priority went to the highest bidder.

The *shochet*, realizing that his selfless offer had not accomplished anything, decided not to postpone his trip any longer. He helped us immeasurably by not revealing his impending departure to his Polish landlord, so that we were able to remain in his apartment. He did me the additional favor of procuring for me some kind of Slovak identity papers, issued to Moshe Elyakim Beriah, a pre-war friend of mine. Although the document was of no great value, psychologically it gave me a tremendous boost.

My future looked quite bleak, but "the Guardian of Israel neither slumbers nor sleeps." Salvation arrived in the person of Avraham Yitzchak Glanzer, a nephew of the *shochet,* also a holder of foreign citizenship papers.

"Don't worry," he told me. "I am friendly with the Pole who runs the escape network. I'll see to it that he takes you in the next transport."

During the course of our conversation, I briefed him on my financial condition. I was carrying cash and the piece of material I had prepared for the Polish policeman, a total value of about one hundred and twenty dollars, which would be sufficient to cover the cost of my escape and that of my friend Herschel and his family. The organization demanded one hundred and fifty dollars for the same rescue operation. Avraham Yitzchak also handed me his uncle's foreign citizenship documents. Since his uncle had already crossed the border, he did not need them any longer, and his passport picture bore a slight resemblance to me. So now I was kosher. Well, not quite, since the local police knew all the foreign nationals personally, but the document gave me a sense of security.

It was around this time that I learned of the horrifying fate that had befallen the people caught in the bunkers in the Bochnia ghetto. After being detained in the *Judenrat* jail, all prisoners were brought to a courtyard where the Germans shot all of them to death. Afterwards, they removed the victims' clothes for the purpose of finding hidden valuables. The bodies were then stacked and burned on a pile of wood which had been prepared by Jewish slave laborers. Two hundred pure and innocent souls, including my dear mother and her two grandchildren, died in the murderous pyre.

A Jewish policeman I knew told me that before the

prisoners were led to their execution, my mother called him over and told him, "I'm well aware of what they are going to do to us. I have only minutes to live, but I'm not afraid to die. I am going to my death as if I were going to a wedding. I am happy mainly because I have been granted the *zchus* of marrying off my children the way I have always hoped for, to decent, Torah-observant husbands and wives. I am also happy that my son Chaim Shlomo and his daughter managed to escape from the ghetto. I fervently hope and pray that they will survive."

Although I knew all along what was in store for the people arrested by the Germans, I was still shocked and outraged upon hearing the report. My mother being killed so brutally deeply saddened me. I was overcome with inconsolable grief. Whoever knew her could attest that she exemplified the verse, A woman of valor, who can find her? (*Mishlei* 31:10) She distinguished herself by her noble character and her deeds of charity and kindness. On the way to her death—as I was told—she did not cry or lament. She accepted her fate with love, with the full knowledge that she was offering her life *al kiddush Hashem*, for the greater glory of Hashem's Name.

The courtyard where they were murdered was situated in the center of Salno Gura Street. The fire department, alerted by the column of smoke rising from the roaring fire, rushed to the scene. However, the German scoundrels sent them back. "It's nothing," they said. "Just a bunch of Jews burning."

During those days of death, destruction and unremitting pain and sorrow, it became increasingly difficult to maintain the level of religious observance with regard to *davening* with a *minyan*, putting on *tefillin*, observing *Shabbos*, *kashrus* and other *mitzvos*. It took immense effort and sacrifice to fulfill the laws of the Torah. Even among the most scrupulously observant Jews, a gradual relaxation of the standards of observance could be noticed, to the point of sliding into an attitude of carefree negligence.

Personally, I experienced great difficulty in observing the *mitzvos,* and I was afraid of becoming accustomed to a life of non-observance. In order to prevent my drifting away from Torah-life, I solemnly resolved never, not even under the worst circumstances, to violate either of the following two *mitzvos.* I would never shave with a straight razor or a razor blade, and I would never eat non-kosher food. I reasoned that it was within my power to observe both of these prohibitions, in contrast to other *mitzvos* where I would be subject to the will of the German oppressors. As I recall, it was these *mitzvos* in particular that created great difficulty for me, but I resisted all temptation.

My first test came about in Prokatzim where I was walking around without papers and without the yellow *Judenstern.* Any spot check would have placed me in mortal danger. In the meantime, my beard began to grow. I had no electric shaver, and of course, a beard was the earmark of a Jew. Moreover, this would present a serious danger when I would have to travel several hours by train to reach the Slovak border. Evaluating my situation I concluded that under these circumstances shaving constituted *pikuach nefesh*—a life saving procedure which is permitted. Consequently, I decided to get a shave with a straight razor. I went to a barber shop, but just as I was about to enter I stopped.

No, I said to myself. I'm not going to do it. I won't violate my vow, no matter what will happen. Hashem can help me anyway, and perhaps He will help me precisely because of my refusal to shave.

I am happy to say that the eventual trip to the border passed without incident, in spite of my beard.

In the meantime, however, I was still stranded in Prokatzim. The appalling news from the Bochnia ghetto and my mother's cruel death shocked me to the core, but there was no time for weeping, not even for sitting *shivah*. My first priority was to save my life and that of my daughter. As long as we were trapped in the German claws our lives were in danger.

My stay in Prokatzim dragged on and on, a buzz of activity with few results. Finally, after waiting for ten days, Avraham Yitzchak told Herschel and me to pack our bags.

"Today you're going to Slovakia," he explained. "The Pole agreed to take you first. The others can wait."

We were ecstatic. At long last, we would escape the lion's den! To be sure, we still had to clear a good many hurdles, but we were confident that Hashem would help us, just as He had saved us until then. We packed our meager possessions, and we were on our way!

At the designated meeting place, we found a fairly large group of people waiting to cross the border together with us. Also present were the Poles who would guide us to our destination, headed by Kortchmartchek, the railroad engineer.

"Today I'm taking only the people who fled from Bochnia," he announced, standing on a chair. "All others go home. I'll take you next time."

The organizers had devised an ingenious plan. The train which would take us from Prokatzim to the Polish-Slovak border was staffed by men who were in on the plot. At the border station, we would be met by people who would lead us across the border in the dark of night. In Prokatzim, the Jews were to be guided by Polish scouts who would survey the road to the station. Kortchmartchek would give the all-clear from the window of the incoming train. In the event that a German inspector boarded the train in Cracow, Kortchmartchek would give a sign and the Jews would head back to wait for another opportunity. For added insurance, they had arranged for Polish women to bring the children to the station and to ride with them to the border.

The reason for selecting the Polish-Slovak border was that German border guards were deployed all along the Polish-Hungarian border, making it virtually impenetrable. At the Slovak border, however, the Germans relied on the high Carpathian Mountains to deter any escape attempt. Reasoning that no one would dare scale the treacherous cliffs, the Germans did not guard this border very heavily. Eventually, the Germans discovered the Slovak escape route, as well as the names of the members of the smugglers' organization. Kortchmartchek, who was on their most wanted list, narrowly escaped to Hungary, where he remained until the war's end.

Before setting out on our journey, we were given several important instructions. One, throughout the entire trip we were not to exhibit any familiarity with our Polish guides, not to speak to them or ask questions. Two, in case someone would get caught, either by the Polish police or by the Germans, he was not to divulge the identity of the escaping Jews or of the members of the organization. Three, all adults were to find seats in different compartments, while the children, accompanied by Polish women would travel in another compartment. Four, upon arrival at the station near the border, we were to proceed straight to the end of the platform where two men would be waiting. We were to follow these men without speaking to them.

A quick wave of Kortchmartchek's hand told us it was time to move. The short walk to the station gave me a sinking feeling in my stomach, since we had to pass the notorious Jerusalemska death camp. Just as we were going by, a group of Jews guarded by "black guards" were working alongside the road. The mere sight of these guards was enough to send shivers down my spine. Feigning indifference, I projected an I-couldn't-care-less image, while my heart was beating rapidly with trepidation. With Hashem's help, everything went smoothly.

While we were waiting at a safe distance from the platform, the Polish women with the children remained on the platform to find out from Kortchmartchek whether it was safe for us to travel. When the train pulled in, I took a seat in a separate compartment, according to instructions, and slowly the train began to move, gradually picking up speed.

One thing troubled me a great deal. Since Sheindl could speak only Yiddish, one word of hers might foul up the entire operation. I pointed this out to the Polish woman taking care of her.

"Don't worry," she reassured me. "I'll see to it that everything turns out all right."

Just to be sure I gave Sheindl some candy to keep her quiet. I paid five hundred *zlotys* for this trip, but it was well worth it.

"Tickets, please," the conductor called out.

I handed him my ticket, but he was not satisfied.

"Let me see your identification," he demanded.

I was terrified. What's this? The entire crew was supposed to be in on the operation. Could this be a new man?

With outward calm, I showed him the foreign papers the *shochet* had left me. The conductor glanced at them.

"Everything's okay," he said.

I breathed an audible sigh of relief.

After a long ride, we arrived at our destination. As soon as we got off, the two men waiting for us on the platform started to march ahead, leading the way. We followed them, and after a long walk, we found ourselves deep in a forest. There was no one else around, nothing to fear.

Before long, Kortchmartchek arrived. He took a head count to make sure no one was missing. There were twelve in our group. One of the guides asked for volunteers who wanted to accomplish the border crossing in one night. He explained that, as a rule, the journey took two nights, and the intervening day was spent in the dense forest.

I myself could hardly wait to put the German misery behind me. Aside from that, there always loomed the possibility that the Germans might attack us. Many times before, when they found out about an escape attempt, they surrounded the forest and ferreted out the unfortunate Jews. I readily agreed to join the guide, and several others, including Herschel, followed suit. Facing a grave predicament, we had nowhere to turn.

CHAPTER 26

■

The Slovak Border

AFTER BIDDING FAREWELL TO THE OTHERS, WE SET OUT on our trek across the border. At first, things went very smoothly, as we marched through fields on a level road. The bright moon smiled at us, and even the pleasant weather seemed to cooperate with us. After marching for a good hour, we took a break. Not bad, not bad at all. Certainly not as bad as I was led to believe it would be. However, as we continued I realized how wrong I was.

We were entering a mountainous region. What had started out as an easy march was turning into an uphill climb. Laboriously, I trudged along, breathing heavily, while Sheindl kept asking for water. My small canteen was empty, and I was forced to draw water from muddy puddles alongside the trail. Never mind cleanliness, the main thing was to keep her quiet, since the slightest sound might betray us.

After several hours of steep climbing, we noticed that our guide, who was marching ahead of us, suddenly doubled back at full speed, motioning to us to follow him. Without asking questions, we followed suit, running at top speed. This was twice as difficult for me, since I was carrying my child. We reached the valley where we crept on hands and knees, seeking shelter among the bushes. There we stayed, trembling with the fear of being discovered.

The reason for our precipitous flight was that the Poles living in this region had begun noticing Jewish groups crossing the border. They would lay in ambush to capture the escaping Jews, either in order to hand them over to the police or simply to extort money from them. Luckily, our guide spotted them first and alerted us.

At long last, the guide ventured out of our hiding place to ascertain if the coast was clear. He gave us the thumbs-up signal, and once again, we plodded up the mountain, scaling sheer cliffs, often hanging on by our nails, until we reached the peak, only to continue on to the next summit. Meanwhile, the moon disappeared, and total darkness shrouded everything. We had to stay close to each other and advance very slowly. The climb seemed endless; my back was aching from carrying Sheindl up the steep incline step by laborious step.

We were approaching the Slovak border in the area dominated by the towering High Tatra Mountains, which soar to heights of seven thousand feet. The mountain trail rose almost perpendicular, straight up. Normal climbing became impossible, and we had to proceed on hands and knees. Straining with all my might, perspiring profusely as I carried Sheindl, I managed to keep up with the group.

After reaching the first high summit, we all collapsed,

totally exhausted and out of breath. Our guide allowed us a short rest period, but not too long, since every minute was precious. But the people were simply too worn-out to get up. Noting the rundown condition of the group, the guide was willing to allow us to spend the night there and continue our trip the following night. Personally, I did not mind going along with his suggestion being that I was absolutely drained. I had tried a variety of methods of carrying the child—on my arms, my back, my shoulders, my head—but now, I was too tired to take even one more step. On the other hand, I reasoned that staying there would be hazardous. We, therefore, asked the guide to let us rest a little longer and then to continue, to which he agreed. With our last ounce of strength, we got up to resume our march. But now our guide changed his tune.

"Whoever doesn't keep up with the group is going to get clobbered," he growled, picking up a heavy stick. "If we get stuck crossing the border, we're all done for."

We made slow but steady progress, climbing mountain after mountain, while our guide goaded us on with his stick.

"Five more kilometers to the border," he announced.

More endless laborious trudging.

"Four more kilometers to the border," he announced.

His tactics worked. Bit by agonizing bit, we closed the distance to the border.

"Listen folks, we're getting close to the border," he finally announced. "Keep quiet, and make sure the children are kept quiet! There's a German checkpoint nearby."

The last sentence started the adrenalin flowing. With newfound energy, we advanced quickly, driven by the notion that each step brought us closer to freedom from the German Kingdom of the Night.

"Hurry up, hurry up," the guide kept urging us on. "Dawn is breaking. Quick!"

Finally, the mountains receded behind us, and we were on flat ground once again. We were really stepping up our pace. A thin red ribbon of light appeared on the horizon. Dawn was breaking. We saw a white border marker . . . and we walked past it.

"*Baruch Hashem!*" I exclaimed loudly, the first words I spoke in freedom.

I breathed a deep sigh of relief. Somehow, freedom became tangible. I felt a sense of buoyancy. I was walking on air.

Meanwhile, we did not slow down but continued marching to the first hamlet, about thirty minutes from the border. Our guide knocked on the door of one of the farmhouses. The door opened, and we all entered. The Slovak farmer quickly brought water for us to freshen up, while at the same time, our guide asked me to sign a paper certifying that he had carried out his mission. I was happy to comply and thanked him for a job well done.

The Slovak family treated us very cordially.

"Now you have nothing to fear any more," the farmer said, smiling graciously. "In the attic, there is plenty of room for you all to rest up."

In the spacious attic, we were served an abundance of food and water. The simple food tasted like a gourmet banquet. After the meal, we bedded down on the fragrant hay, resting our weary bones and relaxing our taut nerves. Feeling an indescribable sense of relief at having escaped the German inferno, I even began to dream that some day I would resume a normal life again.

My joy was short-lived. I had barely rested for a couple of

hours when I heard the sound of heavy boots climbing the stairs to the attic. Seconds later, four men appeared, one dressed in civilian clothes, the others in uniform. They pointed their guns at us.

Here we go again, I thought. The Germans caught up with us after all we've been through!

"Everybody, get up!" they shouted.

Everyone got up. The men searched the hay for valuables but found nothing. In the last minute, right under their noses, I managed to hide the small amount of money I had.

They instructed us to go down into the street. In spite of everything, I was relieved to note that they were, after all, Slovak policemen, not Germans.

"Where are you taking us?" I asked one of the policemen.

"Back to where you came from," he retorted. "Across the border."

I was stunned. Could he be lying? Turning to another policeman who looked Jewish I asked the same question.

"You are being taken by bus to the police station in the village down the road," he replied.

I repeated to him the answer his colleague had just given me.

"Oh, forget it," he said. "He was just kidding."

The good man certainly put my mind at ease. We were instructed to board the waiting bus. One of the policemen escorting us got up.

"Anyone trying to escape will be shot at once," he announced, brandishing his revolver.

Checking my pockets, I tore up any incriminating papers, shredding everything—even family pictures—and threw the pieces out the window.

After a half hour's ride, we came to the police station of

the village of Yablonka. The police inspector invited us to sit down and inquired as to whether we had eaten breakfast. Before long, fresh bread and coffee were served, food I had not seen in a long time. We ate to our heart's content.

After the meal, he interrogated each person individually about his experiences under the Germans. Subsequently, we had to submit to a body search; the women were searched in a separate room by policewomen. All valuables, gold, silver and diamonds were confiscated, as well as less valuable items like watches and fountain pens. At noon, bread and soup were served to anyone wishing to eat. Later that afternoon, we were taken to the bus station under police escort.

"Where are you taking us?" I asked one of the policemen.

"To Hungary," was the laconic answer.

It sounded like a cruel hoax. I had the distinct impression that we were being taken to prison. Feverishly, I tried to devise an escape scheme, but I would have to leave Sheindl behind. Out of the question. I would have to leave my fate in the hands of Hashem.

Towards evening, we arrived at the village of Tristina, where we were led into a large building. A public official squeezed us all into a tiny room. When we asked him for some food and water, he slammed the door shut. Our worst fears were suddenly realized. Here we were, tightly pressed into a suffocating cell without food or drink. The children were crying, and we had nothing to offer them. It was completely dark. There was nothing to do but to try to get some sleep.

Imagine our heartbreak and disappointment. Hunger and pain were things to which we were accustomed, but now we had to cope with the gnawing worry about the future.

"Hashem has helped thus far," we tried to reassure each other. "He will not abandon us now."

Sitting in the dark, each of us was engrossed in his own private thoughts. About two hours later, the lamp hanging from the ceiling was turned on from the outside, and the room was suddenly bathed in bright light. The door opened, and a well-dressed gentleman entered. He was accompanied by the official who had brought us to this room.

"Don't worry," the gentleman said, after inquiring about our situation. "You'll be staying here only for one day. Tomorrow, you continue on to Hungary."

"Are you Jewish?" I asked him, having noticed his small *magen david* lapel pin.

"Yes," was his straightforward answer.

Hearing his message, we became jubilant.

"I'm going to get you some food," he promised.

True to his word, he came back together with his daughter a half hour later, carrying a large basket filled with fresh bread, savory hot roast beef, fruit and several bottles of milk, truly a royal feast. Our mouths were watering.

"Is the meat kosher?" I asked.

"No, it is not," he replied apologetically. "Sorry to say, we have no *shochet*."

We explained that we could not eat the meat and that it would be best if he took it back. He bid us a friendly good-bye and left. The children fell all over the delicious milk, and we sat down to eat the fruit, the likes of which we had not seen since the beginning of the war. Less than thirty minutes later, the daughter came back with a box filled with hard-boiled eggs to replace the roast we had to forgo.

"Tomorrow, I'm coming to visit you again," she said, flashing a warm smile as she turned to leave.

After such a good meal and the happy news, I fell into a deep sleep. The trip to Hungary was not an empty dream after all. It was actually coming true.

Early in the morning, the magnanimous Jewish gentleman and his daughter brought a new supply of food. Only
then did I notice the scribbles on the wall of our small cell
room, written most probably by people who, like us, had
been locked up here. The inscriptions were hope-inspiring
messages addressed to future occupants of this room.

"Don't worry," one of the inscriptions read. "From here
you'll be taken to Hungary."

I recognized many of the signatures as belonging to
Bochnia ghetto inmates who had fled earlier.

The next morning, we were told to go to the courtyard,
where we found people who had been brought there from
other prisons. After breakfast, we marched to the railroad
station escorted by Slovak officers and entered a specially
reserved railroad car. We were on our way! I don't care where
we are going, I thought, as long as we are moving. On the
train, the officers treated us very kindly, sharing their food
with us, offering cigarettes to the men and candy to the
children. After several hours of travelling, we arrived in
Mikolash, where we were greeted by representatives of the
Jewish community who brought us to the community center.

At the community center, we met a large number of
friends and acquaintances, mostly from the Bochnia ghetto
who were waiting to go on to Hungary. Some of them had no
desire at all to leave, since the local Jewish community
provided them with food and shelter. Besides, why should
they jeopardize their life once again? Furthermore, rumor
had it that the Hungarians handed over to the Germans all
refugees they rounded up, and falling into German hands
meant certain death.

The Jewish community gave us a very cordial reception,

taking care of all our needs. Meals were served in a large hall, and several spacious rooms were set aside as sleeping quarters. After a good night's sleep, we were taken back to the police station where they returned to us the small items taken from us in Yablonka, such as the watches and fountain pens. The valuable articles they kept. I took advantage of the opportunity to take Sheindl to a doctor. On our climb across the mountains, she had become ill, but thanks to the medication I now acquired, she soon recovered.

It was only much later that I found out what the Slovak government policy was of dealing with the refugee problem. Upon the intervention of Slovak Jews, the Slovak government agreed to assist the refugees who escaped from Poland and not to hand them over to the Germans, which would amount to a death sentence. A directive was issued to all police precincts, especially to those near the border, not to extradite any Jew who illegally crossed the border. Instead, the directive stated, these Jews were to be detained in a town near the border, in our case Yablonka. The purpose of this procedure was to confiscate the valuables they were carrying on their persons. This was the payoff for their humanitarian treatment of the Jews. It turned out to be a very lucrative enterprise for the Slovaks. Many of the refugees carried their entire fortune in their valise, including diamonds, jewels, pearls and cash. This was the reason for the body search to which we had been subjected. The government even offered a bounty of one thousand Czech *kronen*, a considerable amount, to anyone turning in an illegal Jew.

Now it became clear to me how the police knew at once of our hiding place in the attic. I had been wondering about this all along. The simple answer was that the hospitable farmer at whose farmstead we were staying, tempted by the promised reward of one thousand *kronen* a head, had reported us to the police. By frisking us, the police netted a handsome profit. Indeed, they found a veritable fortune in cash on Yehoshua Weinfeld, a wealthy Cracow industrialist, in addition to the smaller amounts they found on the other members of the group. Having plundered them, the Slovaks wanted to make sure that none of the Jews remained on Slovak territory. For this purpose, each group of refugees was taken under police escort to the Hungarian border.

It is well-known that Rabbi Michoel Ber Weissmandl, the leader of Slovak Jewry, labored throughout the war years with superhuman heroism and self-sacrifice to save Jewish lives from the clutches of the Germans. Rabbi Weissmandl negotiated an arrangement with Dieter Wisliceny, Eichmann's adjutant in Slovakia, to halt the deportations of Slovak Jews indefinitely for a payment of fifty thousand dollars. Later, a deal was negotiated with Eichmann whereby Jewish lives would be traded for trucks. Thousands of Jewish lives could have been saved if leading Jewish figures in America had paid attention to Rabbi Weissmandl's clamors for help. In the end, he himself was arrested by the Germans and placed on a train to Auschwitz. Miraculously, he managed to escape by jumping off the moving train. After surviving the war, he settled in the United States where he established and led an outstanding *yeshivah*. The experiences of the Slovak Jews among whom we had come are well-chronicled in his heartrending autobiography, entitled *Min Hameitzar* (From the Depths), in which he records his negotiations with the Slovak and Nazi chieftains, including Eichmann, and provides copies of the original documents.

CHAPTER 27

■

Budapest at Last

O N FRIDAY MORNING, THE MIKOLASH POLICE INSPECTOR appeared and called out the names of the people scheduled to proceed to Hungary. Hearing my name, I jumped for joy.

"Be ready in ten minutes," we were told.

It took me only a few minutes to pack my baggage; my little daughter represented my entire fortune. Accompanied by police and members of the Jewish community, we marched to the station where we boarded the train. Our group, which comprised twenty-two persons, was assigned a special car.

Moving through a scenic wonderland of majestic mountains and verdant valleys, I sensed a cheerful exhilaration, not strong enough, however, to dispel my uneasiness about what lay ahead.

Without warning, the train came to a halt in the middle of nowhere.

"Everybody, get off!" a shrill voice rang out. "Quickly!"

What was the meaning of this? The train was supposed to take us to Preshov, from where we would be led across the border. Why were we stopping here? But orders are orders. Our group got off, and the train moved on.

"Shalom aleichem!"

The pleasant greeting came from a group of Jewish men and women who had been awaiting us. Speaking in low voices, they indicated to us to speak only in whispers. They showed us two cars that were prepared for us. Since there was not enough room for all of us, we were divided into two groups. I was assigned to the first trip, which made me very happy, thinking that the car would take me across the border into Hungary, that freedom and safety were within arm's reach at last. We had been led to believe that our entry into Hungary would be legal. Unfortunately, there was not a shred of truth to it; the Hungarian government had never agreed to accept any refugees.

During the car ride, I found out the reason for the change of plans. Someone had alerted the government that the Jewish community of Preshov was helping people escape from Poland to Hungary. As a result, they were forced to change the escape route, and we were picked up midway, rather than enter Preshov where the police were waiting to arrest us.

After a ten-minute ride, we got out of the car, and our Slovak guide led us away from the highway into a field, where he told us to wait until the second group would arrive. There was no doubt about it, this border crossing was going to be a replay of our harrowing crossing into Slovakia. But there was nothing I could do about it, except pray that Hashem bring an end to our troubles.

Half an hour later, the cars brought the others. Our two guides told us that our march to Kaschau on the Hungarian side of the border would take no more than two or three hours.

"It's a straight and level road," they reassured us. "It's going to be smooth sailing."

And so it was—until we entered a jungle-like forest. The thick foliage completely blocked out the sun, forcing us to hold hands in order to stay together. This was important, as people would frequently be badly injured on these border crossings by tripping over a fallen branch or stumbling into a hidden hole.

"Stop," our guides called out, as in the distance we recognized six men coming in our direction.

"We are very close to the border now," our guides explained. "These men will lead us across to a nearby village, where we will spend the night. Early in the morning, they will take us to Kaschau."

Since there were too many of us to take across at one time, the guides split us up into groups of four, one guide to each group. Everyone pushed to be in the first group, thinking it would be the most likely to succeed. Sticking to my rule never to force my way into anything, I calmly waited until all the groups were formed.

The first group of six people set out at once, while the others waited to give them a head start. The spacing was done so that, in the event one group was captured, the others would not fall into the same trap.

We sat down and waited, but after five minutes, we suddenly heard the sounds of crying and shrieking in the distance. Obviously, the first group had been captured by the border guards. The wailing and moaning of the unfortunate refugees blended with the shouts of the border guards and the barking of their dogs. The crying and wailing made our hair stand on end; we knew that our friends were doomed. Our guides, who were just as frightened as we were, motioned to us to lie down. Without saying a word, we lay down flat on the ground, the sword of death hanging over our heads.

For an hour and a half, we lay there, until complete silence returned to the forest, a sure sign that the border guards had left. Meanwhile, the five guides who were to lead us to the village all disappeared for fear that they, too, would be caught. Our two guides wanted to follow suit. We implored them not to abandon us here in the middle of the dark forest, but it was no use.

"If they catch us," they argued, "we'll be shot as smugglers. But if you are caught, nothing will happen to you. The Hungarians treat all Jewish refugees very kindly."

We were not taken in by their story. "If you refuse to take us across the border," we said, "then at least take us back to the town from which we came. We cannot possibly stay here."

"If we bring you back, we don't get paid," they replied. "And we need the money."

We begged and cajoled. It was to no avail. They showed us the trail which leads to the border.

"Go straight ahead, then turn right," they said. "After that, turn left."

Before we could ask for more details, they picked themselves up and disappeared.

There we were, alone in the middle of a deep forest, not knowing where to turn. After talking things over, we decided we had no choice but to try to cross the border by ourselves. Soon it would be daylight, which would make our venture even more hazardous.

Setting out in the direction the guides had indicated, we calculated that we would be on Hungarian soil within thirty minutes. However, we lost our way on account of the darkness. We walked and walked without getting anywhere, going around in circles. We felt like a cat chasing its own tail. Were we on Hungarian or Slovak territory? At last, we caught sight of a village in the distance. Assuming it to be a Hungarian village, we made our way towards it. In fact, we reasoned that the city lights we perceived on the horizon must be Kaschau. We became even more convinced when we began to hear the humming of machinery emanating from the factories of the city.

We decided to go to Kaschau by way of the village, since on the bypass we were likely to run into police patrols. As we approached the village, as if on cue, all the dogs welcomed us with earsplitting barks. We quickly retreated for fear of waking up the border guards.

We were at an impasse. How should we proceed? While we were waiting there helplessly, I began to *daven Kabbalas Shabbos*. The same sense of awe I would usually feel at *Kol Nidrei* on *Yom Kippur* gripped me at that moment. I stood there, trembling within. Was this to be my last prayer? After all the hardships and tribulations I had experienced and all the calamities I had suffered, to be caught in this trap within sight of freedom! In spite of these depressing thoughts, I found renewed courage and faith in *Hakadosh Baruch Hu* that this time, too, He would show me a miracle, as He had done until now.

After *davening*, I volunteered to scout the village by

myself to determine the attitude of the peasants towards refugees.

"What have I got to lose?" I argued. "One man will not create as much of a stir as an entire crew of disheveled refugees prancing down Main Street."

I left Sheindl in the care of my friends. She was sleeping soundly in the grass, oblivious to all the goings-on, relying on her father to take care of her. I made my way through the freshly plowed fields to the village, exhausted from all the setbacks and adversities, directing a silent prayer for help to Hashem.

No sooner did I approach the village than the first dog started to bark, arousing the entire dog population into a howling, growling, snarling cacophony. Shrugging off the noise, I advanced into the village. The gate to the first courtyard was closed. I tried the second, the third—they were all closed. I tried a few more houses but still no luck. Since I was not making any headway, I decided to return to the group.

To my surprise, I found them talking to two Hungarians who were on their way to the border. Evidently, they were guides, and my friends had asked them to wait for me. Since I did not speak Hungarian, I had to use sign language to get across to them that we wanted them to lead us to Kaschau. They turned me down, explaining that they had to be in Slovakia that night. After negotiating for half an hour, and promising to make it worth their while, one of them agreed to lead us.

After we marched a good distance, the guide stopped.

"Listen," he said. "I've got to cross into Slovakia tonight, and soon it will be daylight. You can find the way into the city by yourselves. It's easy. I have to go."

We pleaded with him to stay with us, but he vigorously shook his head.

"Nothing doing!" he said.

However, after we promised him five hundred *pengo*, he reconsidered.

When dawn broke, we found ourselves on the outskirts of Kaschau. The city was beginning to stir, people moving in the streets, and our group attracted curious stares. Admittedly, we looked different—to put it mildly. Tired and exhausted, wearing shabby and dirty clothes, carrying tattered bundles and valises, we were a pitiful sight. We rushed our guide, fearful of encountering a police patrol, but he was in no hurry.

"Sit down and wait," he told us.

We were on pins and needles, and he was telling us to wait! At any minute, a policeman was likely to appear. After a short while, however, he told us to continue, as he marched ahead of us along the main thoroughfare. Slowly, the sun was rising and our fears were mounting. I slowed my pace to be last in line, so that if there was trouble I could still run away, but thank Heaven, nothing happened.

The guide took us to the Jewish community building. He rang the bell, but there was no answer; it was still early in the morning. For quite a while, we waited anxiously outside, fearful of being spotted by a passing patrol. At long last, the door opened, and we were ushered inside. We were in the section of the building where the *mikveh* was located. The *gabbaim* welcomed us, brought us into one of the bathrooms and instructed us to stay there for the time being.

Before long, a large crowd of men of all ages began to arrive in order to immerse in the *mikveh*. In the hall, I caught a glimpse of a man with a long white beard and long *peyos*, a sight I had not seen in a long time. I approached him reverently and asked if he served as the rabbi of the community.

"No," he replied. "I'm just an ordinary Jew."

Only then did I recall that in Cracow, too, ordinary Jews had once looked like this, not only rabbis. In the wake of all my grief and troubles, I had almost forgotten what an "ordinary" Jew looked like back home.

It was *Shabbos*, and the *mikveh* building was buzzing with activity. Men wearing long *kapotes*, wide-brimmed hats, their *tzitzis* almost trailing to the floor, were milling about. The majestic scene brought tears to my eyes. A different world— a different planet. These Jews didn't know the meaning of *tzores*, Gestapo, ghettoes, *Aktionen*, massacres, bloodbaths and all the German evils. No fear of Hitler existed here. Only in Poland the sun of life and happiness has been obscured forever by the black smoke of the crematoria.

Within minutes, the *gabbaim* reappeared, carrying platters heaped with an abundance of food and drink—white fresh *challos*, cake and pastries, coffee, milk and butter— everything strictly kosher. The mere sight of all these delicacies breathed new life into our weary bodies.

"Could you find a room where I could put my child to sleep for a while?" I asked one of the men.

"I'm sorry, but that's impossible," he answered resolutely. "You see, anyone caught harboring an illegal immigrant is sent to Poland along with his guest. And no one comes back alive from there."

"So be it," I said to myself. "At least, I have escaped the German hell." Or so I thought.

Regaining my strength after some coffee and cake, I entered the *shul* in the community building where the *Shabbos* service was already in progress. A large number of worshipers were singing happy *niggunim* in an exhilarated mood, while I stood in a corner listening with a broken heart. But how could they be of any help to me?

After *davening*, I had a little talk with the *gabbai*, a very dignified gentleman by the name of Goldstein. To my great delight, he told me that the Belzer Rebbe was in Budapest. He also explained that staying in Kaschau would be extremely dangerous for me. Since Kaschau was close to the border, any illegal Jew snatched by the police was immediately expelled to Poland and, needless to say, the fate that awaited him there.

Listening to him speak, I saw my hopes turn to ashes. I had imagined that my troubles were over now that I was on Hungarian soil, yet my life apparently was still in very real danger. According to Goldstein, plainclothesmen were patrolling the streets looking for illegal aliens whom they detected without much effort. Since aliens did not speak Hungarian, it took only a few short questions to establish their illegal status. He advised me to get to Budapest as soon as possible.

"There you will be safe," he said. "There they have ways of legalizing your status."

In view of the danger that remaining in Kaschau entailed, I decided to indeed go on to Budapest as soon as possible. The Jewish community also was interested in seeing us leave, as sheltering illegal refugees exposed them to grave danger. They informed me that at one o'clock in the afternoon a bus was leaving for Shatra Ujhel. From there, I could catch a connecting train straight to Budapest.

I went along with their suggestion; the main thing was to leave town. At the conclusion of *davening*, we were served an elaborate *Shabbos seudah*—in the *mikveh,* of all places. There was an abundance of all the traditional *Shabbos* dishes, *challos,* fish, meat, *cholent* and *kugel,* a real feast. Only a nagging sense of fear and anxiety marred my enjoyment. On the other hand, my firm trust in Hashem gave me courage to face the uncertain future.

The question was, what to do with Sheindl? A grown man travelling with a small child was bound to arouse suspicion. After a brief discussion, the leaders of the community suggested that my daughter remain in their care for the time being.

"We will place her in the Jewish Children's Home," they assured me. "Whenever you will notify us, we will see to it that she is brought to Budapest."

It seemed like an ideal solution. First, my journey to Budapest was going to be dangerous. Second, having no friends or relatives in Budapest I would have great difficulty finding food and shelter. This was the answer to my problems, or so I thought.

But the plan had a catch. They explained that they would take the child to the police where they would file a deposition to the effect that she had been found in the street. The police would register her as an abandoned child which would give her legal status, whereupon she would be remanded to the custody of the Jewish child care institution.

I did not like this arrangement at all. Although at the present no children were expelled to Poland, who could be sure that this policy would not change? However, having no choice, I agreed. Now I had to persuade Sheindl, who was all of three years old at the time, to go along with the plan. When she realized I was about to leave her, she broke into uncontrollable sobs, clinging to me with all her might. I tried various ways to appease her, but nothing worked. In the end, I placed the totally exhausted child on a bench where she fell asleep. I was ready to set out on my journey.

The *yeshivah* students who were the main organizers of the escape committee immediately went to buy tickets. They could obtain only three train tickets which they assigned to me, Herschel and a third person. The other members of our group would travel straight to Budapest on Sunday. Herschel, however, refused to travel without his family. I tried to point out to him the danger involved in travelling with a small child, but he refused to listen, preferring to wait for the next trip. Someone else took his place.

As we were preparing to leave, the good people of Kaschau gave us a number of instructions and warnings. We were not likely to encounter any secret police at the bus station, since they were active mainly at the railroad station. Nevertheless, since we did not speak Hungarian, we were easy prey. Therefore, the community provided a guide to accompany us so that we would not have to ask for directions. They warned us strongly not to initiate any contact with the guide throughout the entire trip, just to follow him without saying a word. He would take care of everything we needed, such as buying our tickets and other necessities. We were introduced to him, and after expressing our heartfelt thanks for the community's gracious hospitality, we were on our way.

Promptly at one o'clock, the bus left. We were still quite petrified; our pale faces and disheveled clothes gave us away, and we stood out like sore thumbs among the well-dressed passengers on the bus. We tried to look calm and casual, and although terribly tired, we fought off our sleepiness to avoid arousing even the slightest suspicion.

I gazed through the window as we passed through the towns and villages, and I saw a dream world unfolding before my eyes. Jews were calmly taking *Shabbos* afternoon strolls in the company of their families, content after a beautiful *Shabbos* meal.

Look at me, I thought. All my loved ones have been murdered, gassed, burned. Only I and my little girl are left, and even we still need a miracle to stay alive.

After a few hours, we arrived in Shatra Ujhel where we had to catch the train to Budapest. The Shatra Ujhel station was not a healthy place for people like us. The police often conducted raids there in an attempt to find illegal aliens. Silently, we followed our guide as he bought tickets for us, whereupon we boarded the jam-packed train. It was standing-room only, but in spite of the crowding, our appearance piqued the curious interest of the passengers. One distinguished-looking man in particular could not take his eyes off us. We were afraid that he might report us, or that perhaps he was an undercover agent. To avoid his stares, we dispersed to different corners of the car. When he got off at the next station, we all breathed a collective sigh of relief.

Gradually, the train emptied until we even found seats. I sat down briefly, yet in spite of my fatigue I got up for fear that someone might strike up a conversation with me in Hungarian. To make things worse, next to me were seated two Hungarian officers in dress uniform, wearing some kind of top hat decorated with a feathery plume. As I was to learn later, these were officers of the internal security police force called *zsandars*, which means law enforcement officers. Its members were selected from among the young and uneducated peasant boys and received special training in the various techniques of forcing people to talk. By employing crude methods of torture, they were usually able to extract information from prisoners. Often, the victims would die as a result of the brutal beatings. At this moment, however, as I had the honor of sitting next to them, I had no inkling of their expertise. Thus, I got up, placed myself in front of a window and looked out. Meanwhile, the sun began to set, and dusk afforded me more protection. I sang to myself the *zemiros* of *shalosh seudos*, looking forward to our arrival in Budapest.

It was nine o'clock in the evening when the train finally pulled into the Budapest station. The hustle and bustle of thousands of passengers scurrying in all directions made my head swim. Trains arriving, trains departing, clanging, whistling, the blaring music of the radio, the echoing sound of the announcements, the blinding floodlights, all of it left me in a daze. During the years I was locked up in the ghetto, these things had faded from my memory, so that now I felt as though I had suddenly been thrust into a new world.

But never mind the noise and the chaos. I had to keep a cool head and concentrate on following the guide. He led us out onto the plaza where we boarded a streetcar. For the first time, I felt a degree of relief, realizing that we were in Budapest and out of danger.

We got off at Kiray Street where our guide took us to the home of Mr. Schweitzer, one of the wealthy and prominent members of the community and a leading figure in the Jewish Relief Committee for refugees from Poland. At the door, we were met by Mr. Yaker, a member of the refugee organization. Our guide, having fulfilled his mission, was assured of our gratitude for a job well done.

Mr. Schweitzer was a prosperous furrier, but his greatest claim to fame was his dedicated work on behalf of Polish refugees from Nazi terror. His faithful partner in all his undertakings was his noble wife who opened her home to anyone needing help. She was particularly active in relieving the plight of orphans whose parents had been killed by the Germans, feeding and clothing them in the children's home she headed. Like a compassionate mother, she took care of my little Sheindl when I eventually brought her to Budapest, finding a place for her in the children's home. She was ably assisted by two volunteer communal workers, Mr. Yaker and Mr. Turkeltaub, both of whom settled in the United States after the war. Thus it was that I met Mr. Yaker in the Schweitzer home on the first night of my arrival in Budapest.

To my utter surprise and delight, Mr. Yaker informed me that the Belzer Rebbe lived on the same street, only a short distance away.

"But you're wasting your time going there," he said. "There is such a huge crowd waiting to see the Rebbe, they have placed doorkeepers at the entrance. No one is allowed in. Take my advice. Have a bite to eat, and get some sleep."

But I simply could not wait to visit my revered Rebbe.

"Food and sleep don't mean a thing to me unless I first go and see the Rebbe," I insisted.

Seeing that I was not going to be dissuaded, he agreed to take me to the Rebbe's house. Because of the late hour, the official doorkeepers had already gone home, and there were just a few *chassidim* keeping order in front of the Rebbe's residence. They allowed us to enter, although I did not even identify myself, and I proceeded at once toward the room where the Rebbe was presiding over a large crowd of *chassidim* assembled for *shalosh seudos*. This time, I was stopped by the doorkeepers who adamantly refused to let me in. I recognized the doorkeepers from pre-war days when they used to come to Belz, but they did not recognize me. I tried to force my way in, but the guard blocked my way.

"No one is allowed to enter!" he shouted.

The Bilgorayer Rav, the Belzer Rebbe's brother, was seated by the Rebbe's side, and he got up to see what the commotion was all about. He immediately recognized me and whispered to the Rebbe that it was I who was standing at the door. Upon receiving the news, the Rebbe rose from his seat and riveted his eyes on me. Instantly, the wall of guards opened up, and I entered the room. As I walked in, word spread about who I was. The joy radiating from the Rebbe's face was simply beyond words. Everyone had heard of the final *Aktion* in the Bochnia ghetto and that in the end every last inhabitant had been killed. They thought that the same fate had befallen me.

I was deeply moved by the scene I was witnessing, a vision I had not seen in so many years that it took on an otherworldly appearance. The Rebbe, his face beaming with pure holiness, was seated at the head of the table, surrounded by *chassidim* with long beards and *peyos*, dressed in black silk *kapotes*, singing *Yetzaveh Tzur Chasdo* (May the Rock Command His Kindness) to the familiar Belzer *niggun*. Tears welled up in my eyes and streamed freely down my cheeks. I did not wipe them away. They were tears of joy, tears of thanksgiving, of song and praise to Hashem for bringing me to this moment.

After *Havdalah*, the Rebbe invited me to his private chamber. Greeting me with a warm *shalom aleichem*, he asked me in great detail about all my experiences on my journey from Bochnia to Budapest. I did not leave out anything, describing to him, as accurately as I could, all the events I had lived through, with particular attention to my crossing the Hungarian border and how, when we were almost at the end of our rope, a Hungarian peasant appeared who led us into Kaschau.

"*Mamesh malachim haben dich gebrengt!*" the Rebbe exclaimed with holy fervor when I finished my account. "These were real angels that accompanied you!"

He then asked me whether I had brought his *tefillin*, which he had left with me when he escaped to Hungary.

"No," I replied.

"Did you bring your own *tefillin?*"

"No, I couldn't bring those either," I replied. "But I did carry in my valise a few pages of hand-written Torah commentaries by the Rebbe."

"Did you really?" the Rebbe asked, jumping out of his seat with excitement. "Tell me, where are they?"

Fleeing from Bochnia, I had thrown away all papers that might betray my Jewish identity, but this manuscript I guarded like the priceless treasure which it truly was. I believed that the moment would come that I would see the Rebbe again and hand it over to him. At the same time, I felt sure that the merit of this manuscript would help me to overcome all adversity and arrive safely in Hungary. Now, I pulled the precious pages out of my breast pocket and placed them on the table. The Rebbe was overjoyed at seeing his manuscript.

"*Die hast mich mamesh mechayeh geven!*" he exclaimed. "You truly gave me a new lease on life!"

The Rebbe invited me to stay at his house and instructed his household to treat me like an honored guest. To begin with, I was served a full *melaveh malkah* meal, and for the following four months, until the Rebbe's departure for Eretz Yisrael, I found a haven at the Rebbe's house.

Of course, I could not spend the nights there, so I had to find a place to sleep. Luckily, however, I ran into a friend who had come to visit the Rebbe. Since he was returning home that night, he offered me his room in the Jewish hotel for which he had paid in advance. The hotelkeeper, noticing that I was a foreigner, was reluctant to let me stay at the hotel. Meanwhile, his entire family—his wife and children—gathered to stare at this strange creature from outer space who did not speak Hungarian. Their unanimous decision was that a character like this should not be admitted to their hotel. There was nothing left for me to do but go sleep on a park bench.

A few days later, I received grim news about the fate of the other members of our group. According to the report, several people, including Herschel and his family, left Kaschau by train on Sunday. They were captured by the police, deported back to Poland and handed over to the Germans, who killed them on the spot. It was Hashem's guiding Hand that had prompted me to leave on the earlier trip. Praise to Hashem for delivering me from my pursuers who wanted to take my life.

Chaim Shlomo Friedman spent the rest of the war in Hungary, ending many harrowing experiences before it was over. With great difficulty he located and was reunited with his daughter after the war was over. He remarried and settled in Antwerp, where he raised an exemplary family of eight children—five sons and three daughters—all of whom now have families of their own which follow in their grandfather's tradition of Torah, yiras shamayim and chassidus. After a fruitful and rewarding life, the author passed away on 25 Tishrei, 5746 (1985), at the age of seventy-two and was laid to rest in Yerushalayim.

May his stunning memoir be an everlasting legacy of unflinching emunah and bitachon for future generations.